Richard Lovelace

Shearsman Classics Vol. XXVI

Other titles in the *Shearsman Classics* series:

1. *Poets of Devon and Cornwall, from Barclay to Coleridge* (2007)
2. Robert Herrick *Selected Poems* (2007)
3. *Spanish Poetry of the Golden Age, in contemporary English translations* (2008)
4. Mary, Lady Chudleigh *Selected Poems* (2009)
5. William Strode *Selected Poems* (2009)
6. Sir Thomas Wyatt *Selected Poems* (2010)
7. *Tottel's Miscellany* (1557)   (The Tudor Miscellanies, Vol. 1) (2010)
8. *The Phœnix Nest* (1593)   (The Tudor Miscellanies, Vol. 2) (2010)
9. *Englands Helicon* (1600)   (The Tudor Miscellanies, Vol. 3) (2010)
10. Mary Coleridge *Selected Poems* (2010)
11. D.H. Lawrence *Look! We Have Come Through!* (2011)
12. D.H. Lawrence *Birds, Beasts and Flowers* (2011)
13. D.H. Lawrence *Studies in Classic American Literature* (2011)
14. Johann Wolfgang von Goethe *Faust* (translated by Mike Smith) (2012)
15. Robert Browning *Dramatic Romances* (2012)
16. Robert Browning *Sordello* (2012)
17. Robert Browning *The Ring and the Book* (2012)
18. Fernando de Herrera *Selected Poems*
      (translated by Luis Ingelmo & Michael Smith) (2014)
19. Thomas Gray *The English Poems* (2014)
20. Antonio Machado *Solitudes & Other Early Poems*
      (translated by Michael Smith & Luis Ingelmo) (2015)
21. John Donne *Poems (1633)* (2015)
22. Thomas Carew *Collected Poems* (2015)
23. Gerard Manley Hopkins *The Wreck of the Deutschland* (ed. Nigel Foxell) (2017)
24. Gérard de Nerval *Les Chimères* (translated by Will Stone) (2017)
25. Sir John Suckling *Collected Poems* (2020)
26. Richard Lovelace *Collected Poems* (2020)
27. Robert Herrick *Hesperides (1648)* (2018)
28. Algernon Charles Swinburne *Our Lady of Pain: Poems of Eros and Perversion*
      (edited by Mark Scroggins) (2019)
29. Luís Vaz de Camões *The Lusiad* (trans. by Sir Richard Fanshawe, 1666) (2020)
30. Luís Vaz de Camões *Selected Shorter Poems* (trans. by Jonathan Griffin) (2020)

The Collected Poems

of

Richard Lovelace

Shearsman Books

First published in the United Kingdom in 2020 by
Shearsman Books Ltd
PO Box 4239
Swindon
SN3 9FN

Shearsman Books Ltd Registered Office
3 – 1 St. James Place, Mangotsfield, Bristol BS16 9JB
(this address not for correspondence)

www.shearsman.com

Shearsman Classics Vol. 26

ISBN 978-1-84861-617-2

Notes and editorial matter
copyright © Shearsman Books Ltd, 2020

Contents

Introduction / 9

To the Right Hon. my Lady Anne Lovelace / 13

Song. To Lucasta, *Going beyond the Seas* / 15
Song. To Lucasta, Going to the Warre / 16
A Paradox / 16
Song. To Amarantha, *That she would dishevell her haire* / 18
To Chloe, *Courting her for his Friend* / 19
Sonnet / 20
Ode. To Lucasta. *The Rose* / 21
Gratiana *dauncing and singing* / 22
The Scrutinie. Song / 23
Princesse Löysa *drawing* / 24
An Elegie. *Princesse* Katherine… / 25
Love Conquer'd. A Song / 27
A loose Saraband / 28
A forsaken Lady to her false Servant… / 30
Orpheus *to* Beasts. Song / 32
Orpheus *to* Woods. Song / 32
The Grasse-hopper. Ode / 33
Dialogue. Lucasta, Alexis / 35
To Ellinda, That lately I have not written / 37
Sonnet / 37
Lucasta Weeping. Song / 38
The Vintage to the Dungeon. A Song / 39
On the Death of Mrs. Elizabeth Filmer / 39
To Lucasta. From Prison. An Epode / 41
Lucasta's Fanne, With a Looking glasse in it / 43
Lucasta, taking the waters at Tunbridge. Ode / 45
To Lucasta. Ode Lyrick / 46
To my Worthy Friend Mr. Peter Lilly… / 48
Elinda's Glove. Sonnet / 49
To Fletcher reviv'd / 50
The Lady A. L. My Asylum in a great extremity / 52
A Prologue to the Scholars… / 55
—The Epilogue / 56

Clitophon and Lucippe translated. To the Ladies / 57
To my truely valiant, learned Friend, who in his booke
resolv'd the Art Gladiatory into the Mathematick's / 59
Amyntor's Grove. An Elogie / 59
Against the Love of Great Ones / 63
Lucasta paying her Obsequies to the Chast
memory of my dearest Cosin Mrs. Bowes Barne / 65
To Althea. From Prison / 66
Being treated. To Ellinda / 67
Sonnet. To Generall Goring, after the pacification at Berwicke / 68
Sir Thomas Wortley's Sonnet Answered. The Sonnet / 69
The Answer / 70
A Guiltlesse Lady Imprisoned: After Penanced. Song / 71
Upon the Curtaine of Lucasta's Picture, it was thus wrought / 72
To his Deare Brother Colonel F. L.... / 73
An Elegie On the Death of Mrs. Cassandra Cotton... / 74
Lucasta's World. Epode / 76
To a Lady that desired me I would beare my part
with her in a song. Madam A. L. / 77
Valiant Love / 79
The Apostacy of one, and but one Lady / 80
To My Lady H. Ode / 81
La Bella Bona Roba / 82
A La Bourbon... / 83
The Fair Beggar / 83
To Ellinda upon his late recovery. A Paradox / 85
Amyntor from Beyond the Sea to Alexis. A Dialogue / 86
A Lady with a Falcon on her fist / 88
Calling Lucasta from Her Retirement. Ode / 90
Aramantha. A Pastorall / 91

Lucasta: Posthume Poems

Her Reserved Looks / 102
Lucasta Laughing / 102
Song / 103
In Allusion to the French Song
'N'entendez vous pas ce langage' / 103
Night. To Lucasta / 105
Love Inthron'd. Ode / 106
Her Muffe / 107
A Black Patch On Lucasta's Face / 108
Another / 109
To Lucasta I / 110
To Lucasta II / 110
Lucasta At The Bath / 111
The Ant / 112
The Snail / 114
Another / 116
Courante Monsieur / 117
A Loose Saraband / 117
The Falcon / 119
Love made in the first age: To Chloris / 122
To a Lady with child that ask'd an old Shirt / 124
Song / 125
Another / 126
Ode / 126
The Duell / 128
Cupid Far Gone / 129
A Mock-Song / 130
A Fly Caught in a Cobweb / 131
A Fly about a Glasse of Burnt Claret / 132
Female Glory / 135
A Dialogue. Lute and Voice / 135
A Mock Charon. Dialogue / 136
The Toad and Spyder. A Duell / 137
The Triumphs of Philamore and Amoret / 143
Advice to my Best Brother, Coll: Francis Lovelace / 147
An Anniversary: On the Hymeneals of
my Noble Kinsman, Tho. Stanley, Esquire / 150

Paris's Second Judgement… / 151
A Panegyrick to the Best Picture of Friendship, Mr. Pet. Lilly / 151
To my Dear Friend Mr. E[ldred] R[evett]
on His Poems Moral and Divine / 155
To my Noble Kinsman Thomas Stanley… / 157
On the Best, Last, and Only Remaining Comedy of
Mr. Fletcher, *The Wild Goose Chase* / 158
To Dr. F. Beale; on His Book of Chesse / 160
To the Genius of Mr. John Hall
on His Exact Translation of Hierocles… / 160
On Sanazar's Being Honoured… A Satyre / 162

Notes / 171

Introduction

Richard Lovelace – whose name was pronounced *Lóveless*, a fact with which he played at times in his poetry – was born in Woolwich in 1618 into a long-established Kentish family of substantial means, and holders of the manor of Bethersden since 1367. His father Sir William Lovelace was knighted by James I and, like many others of the gentry at that time, had served in the Netherlandish wars, and was to lose his life in action in 1627.

Young Richard was educated at Charterhouse School and at Gloucester Hall, Oxford. His wit and good looks earned him much attention, and his comedy, *The Scholar*, was performed at Oxford in 1636. King Charles I and Queen Henrietta took to him so much that they had him made an M.A. during the royal visit to Oxford that same year. Richard moved on to the Inns of Court in London – a typical right of passage for up-and-coming young men of the day, for whom it was a mixture of postgraduate study and finishing school – and then took up a junior position in the Caroline court. He was taken under the wing of George, Lord Goring, later the Earl of Norwich, and took part in the latter's unsuccessful military campaigns in Scotland in 1639 and 1640. Those campaigns having come to naught, he withdrew to his Kentish estates, where he was to stay until 1642.

In 1642, Lovelace presented a petition to Parliament – at the request of the Kentish supporters of the King, some 500 of whom, bearing arms, accompanied him – in support of the full restoration of the King's rights. By so doing he thus ranked himself with other significant Royalists, and made himself a marked man. Lovelace was imprisoned in Westminster Gatehouse from April 30 to June 21, 1642, and, while behind bars, wrote 'To Althea. From Prison' which includes the words that will forever bear his name: "Stone walls do not a prison make, nor iron bars a cage." 'To Althea' made his literary name and kept it alive long past his natural span of years. His release was on bail of £10,000 – a huge sum – under the surety of two Kentish landowners Thomas Flood and William Clarke.

Upon his release, Lovelace stayed for a while in London, moving in literary and artistic circles, where he became friendly with William Lawes, who was to set a number of poems to music, as well as Sir John Suckling, and then moved abroad, first to the Netherlands and then to France, most likely with Goring, until after King Charles' arrest in 1646.

Lovelace was wounded at the Battle of Dunkirk, and then returned to interregnum England in 1647. He was arrested again by order of Parliament and confined to Peterhouse Prison, Aldersgate, in October 1648, most likely because of his activities against the new regime. After his release in April 1649, Lovelace published his first book of poems, *Lucasta*. The eponymous Lucasta was Lucy Sacherevell, whom Lovelace gave the pet appellation, *Lux casta* [Chaste Light]. Sadly for Richard, Lucy had believed him dead of his wounds at Dunkirk, and had gone on to marry another man.

Lovelace was driven to financial ruin by his support of the King and the Royalist cause, and subsequently depended on the charity of others, only to die in poverty in 1657 at the age of only 39, having been lodging in Gunpowder Lane, an area of poor reputation, off Fleet Street. He was buried at St. Bride's, London – the church was later destroyed in the Great Fire of London. A year after his death, his friends saw to the publication of his remaining poems under the title *Lucasta: Posthume Poems*, the editing of the volume having been carried out by Lovelace's youngest brother, Dudley.

So, Lovelace was a man of talent, socially adept, and well-educated in the manner of his time and class. Under another King he might not have had such quick preferment, but he would also have kept his health, fortune and, indeed, his life. What we have of him now is a solid corpus of poems, typical of the Caroline poets whom one would rank a level below earlier figures such as Jonson and Donne, or contemporaries such as Milton (ten years his senior, and his political opposite) and Marvell (three years his junior, and likewise more attuned to the political currents of the day).

More in line with Lovelace was Sir John Suckling, nine years his senior, a similar witty Royalist with a fine ear and a talent for verse, who perished in France, an apparent suicide, in 1641. A volume of Suckling's *Collected Poems* are being published in tandem with this volume. Suckling would have been one of his comrades during the undistinguished Scottish campaign.

There is no really up-to-date edition of Lovelace's poems – the last major survey came from Oxford University Press, in their Oxford English Texts series, published in two volumes in 1925, and then in a handier one-volume format in 1930. The latter was reprinted in corrected versions several times, the most recent in 1968, as far as I am able to ascertain. The text here follows that edition in cases of doubt. Facsimiles of the first editions of *Lucasta* and *Lucasta: Posthume Poems* were also consulted during the preparation of this volume. The text here has not been modernised – our standard practice where a good edition is no longer in print. The only exceptions to this rule have been to abandon the old "long S" in favour of its modern iteration, the replacement of VV with modern W, and to expand period abbreviations, such as wth for *with*.

Tony Frazer
June 2020

THE DEDICATION

To the Right Honourable, my Lady

ANNE LOVELACE

To the Richest TREASURY
   That e'er fill'd Ambitious Eye;
To the faire bright MAGAZIN
Hath impoverisht Love's Queen;
To th' EXCHEQUER of all honour
(All take Pensions but from her);
To the TAPER of the Thore
Which the god himselfe but bore;
To the SEA of Chast Delight;
Let me cast the DROP I write.
And as at LORETTO's shrine
CÆSAR shovels in his Mine,
Th' Empres spreads her Carkanets,
The lords submit their Coronets,
Knights their Chased Armes hang by,
Maids Diamond-Ruby Fancies tye;
Whilst from the PILGRIM she wears
One poore false Pearl, but ten true tears:
So among the Orient Prize,
(Saphyr-Onyx Eulogies)
Offer'd up unto your fame,
Take my GARNET-DUBLET Name,
And vouchsafe 'midst those rich joyes
(With Devotion) these TOYES.
                      Richard Lovelace.

Song.
Set by Mr. Henry Lawes.

To Lucasta,
Going beyond the Seas

I.

If to be absent were to be
    Away from thee;
  Or that when I am gone,
  You or I were alone;
Then my *Lucasta* might I crave
Pity from blustring winde, or swallowing wave.

II.

But I'le not sigh one blast or gale
    To swell my saile,
  Or pay a teare to swage
  The foaming blew-Gods rage;
For whether he will let me passe
Or no, I'm still as happy as I was.

III.

Though Seas and Land betwixt us both,
    Our Faith and Troth,
  Like separated soules,
  All time and space controules:
Above the highest sphere wee meet
Unseene, unknowne, and greet as Angels greet.

IV.

So then we doe anticipate
    Our after-fate,
  And are alive i' th' skies,
  If thus our lips and eyes
Can speake like spirits unconfin'd
In Heav'n, their earthy bodies left behind.

Song.
Set by Mr. *John Laniere.*

To Lucasta,
Going to the Warres.

I.

Tell me not (Sweet) I am unkinde,
  That from the Nunnerie
Of thy chaste breast, and quiet minde,
  To Warre and Armes I flie.

II.

True; a new Mistresse now I chase,
  The first Foe in the Field;
And with a stronger Faith imbrace
  A Sword, a Horse, a Shield.

III.

Yet this Inconstancy is such,
  As you too shall adore;
I could not love thee (Deare) so much,
  Lov'd I not Honour more.

A Paradox

I.

'Tis true the beauteous Starre
  To which I first did bow
Burnt quicker, brighter far
  Then that which leads me now;
    Which shines with more delight:
    For gazing on that light
    So long, neere lost my sight.

II.

Through foule, we follow
    For had the World one face
And Earth been bright as Ayre,
   We had knowne neither place;
     Indians smell not their Neast:
     A *Swisse* or *Finne* tastes best,
     The Spices of the East.

III.

So from the glorious Sunne,
    Who to his height hath got,
With what delight we runne
   To some black Cave, or Grot!
     And Heav'nly *Sydney* you
     Twice read, had rather view
     Some odde *Romance*, so new.

IV.

The God that constant keepes
    Unto his Dieties,
Is poore in Joyes, and sleepes
   Imprison'd in the skies:
     This knew the wisest, who
     From *Juno* stole, below
     To love a Beare, or Cow.

Song
Set by Mr. *Henry Lawes*

To Amarantha,
That she would dishevell her haire

I

*A*marantha sweet and faire,
  Ah brade no more that shining haire!
  As my curious hand or eye,
Hovering round thee let it flye.

II

  Let it flye as unconfin'd
As its calme Ravisher, the winde;
  Who hath left his darling th' East,
To wanton o're that spicie Neast.

III

  Ev'ry Tresse must be confest;
But neatly tangled at the best;
  Like a Clue of golden thread,
Most excellently ravelled.

IV

  Doe not then winde up that light
In Ribands, and o're-cloud in Night;
  Like the Sun in's early ray,
But shake your head and scatter day.

V

  See 'tis broke! Within this Grove
The Bower, and the walkes of Love,
  Weary lye we downe and rest,
And fanne each others panting breast.

VI

Heere wee'l strippe and coole our fire
In Creame below, in milke-baths higher:
    And when all Well's are drawne dry,
I'le drink a tear out of thine eye.

VII

Which our very Joyes shall leave
That sorrowes thus we can deceive;
    Or our very sorrowes weepe,
That joyes so ripe, so little keepe.

To Chloe,
Courting her for his Friend.

I

*C*hloe behold! againe I bowe,
Againe possest, againe I woe;
    From my heat hath taken fire,
        Damas, noble youth, and fries:
        Gazing with one of mine eyes
    Damas, halfe of me expires:
Chloe, behold! Our Fate's the same,
Or make me Cinders too, or quench his Flame.

II

I'd not be King, unlesse there sate
Lesse Lords that shar'd with me in State;
    Who by their cheaper Coronets know
    What glories from my Diadem flow:
    It's use and rate values the Gem,
    Pearles in their shells have no esteem;
And I being Sun within thy Sphere,
'Tis my chiefe beauty thinner lights shine there.

III

The Us'rer heaps unto his store,
By seeing others praise it more;
    Who not for gaine, or want doth covet,
    But 'cause another loves, doth love it:
    Thus gluttons cloy'd afresh invite
    Their Gusts, from some new appetite;
And after cloth remov'd, and meate,
Fall too againe by seeing others eate.

Sonnet
Set by Mr. *Hudson*

I.

Depose your finger of that Ring,
    And Crowne mine with't awhile
Now I restor't—Pray, do's it bring
    Back with it more of soile?
Or shines it not as innocent,
  As honest, as before 'twas lent?

II.

So then inrich me with that Treasure,
    Will but increase your store,
And please me (faire one) with that pleasure
    Must please you still the more:
Not to save others is a curse
The blackest, when y'are ne're the worse.

Ode.
Set by Dr. *John Wilson*

To Lucasta

The Rose

I.
Sweet serene skye-like Flower,
Haste to adorn her Bower:
    From thy long clowdy bed,
    Shoot forth thy damaske head.

II.
New-startled blush of *Flora!*
The griefe of pale *Aurora*,
    Who will contest no more;
    Haste, haste, to strowe her floore.

III.
Vermilion Ball that's given
From lip to lip in Heaven;
    Love's Couches cover-led:
    Haste, haste, to make her bed.

IV.
Dear Offspring of pleas'd *Venus*,
And Jollie, plumpe *Silenus;*
    Haste, haste, to decke the Haire
    Of th' only, sweetly Faire.

V.
See! Rosie is her Bower,
Her floore is all this Flower;
    Her Bed a Rosie nest
    By a Bed of Roses prest.

VI.

But early as she dresses,
Why fly you her bright Tresses?
    Ah! I have found I feare;
    Because her Cheekes are neere.

Gratiana *dauncing and singing*

I.

See! with what constant Motion
Even, and glorious, as the Sunne,
    Gratiana steeres that Noble Frame,
Soft as her breast, sweet as her voyce
That gave each winding Law and poyze,
    And swifter then the wings of Fame.

II.

She beat the happy Pavement
By such a Starre made Firmament,
    Which now no more the Roofe envies;
But swells up high with *Atlas* ev'n
Bearing the brighter, nobler Heav'n,
    And in her, all the Dieties.

III.

Each step trod out a Lovers thought
And the Ambitious hopes he brought,
    Chain'd to her brave feet with such arts;
Such sweet command, and gentle awe,
As when she ceas'd, we sighing saw
    The floore lay pav'd with broken hearts.

IV.

So did she move; so did she sing
Like the Harmonious spheres that bring
    Unto their Rounds their musick's ayd;

Which she performed such a way,
As all th' inamour'd world will say
   The *Graces* daunced, and *Apollo* play'd.

The Scrutinie
Song
Set by Mr. *Thomas Charles*

I.
Why should you sweare I am forsworn,
   Since thine I vow'd to be?
Lady it is already Morn,
   And 'twas last night I swore to thee
That fond impossibility.

II.
Have I not lov'd thee much and long,
   A tedious twelve houres space?
I must all other Beauties wrong,
   And rob thee of a new imbrace;
Could I still dote upon thy Face.

III.
Not, but all joy in thy browne haire,
   By others may be found;
But I must search the black and faire
   Like skilfull Minerallist's that sound
For Treasure in un-plow'd-up ground.

IV.
Then, if when I have lov'd my round,
   Thou prov'st the pleasant she;
With spoyles of meaner Beauties crown'd,
   I laden will returne to thee,
Ev'n sated with Varietie.

Princesse Löysa *drawing*

I saw a little Diety,
Minerva in Epitomy,
Whom *Venus* at first blush, surpris'd,
Tooke for her winged wagge disguis'd;
But viewing then whereas she made
Not a distrest, but lively shade
Of *Eccho* whom he had betrayd,
Now wanton, and ith' coole oth' Sunne
With her delight a hunting gone;
And thousands more, whom he had slaine,
To live, and love, belov'd againe:
Ah this is true Divinity!
I will un-God that Toye cri'd she?
Then markt she *Syrinx* running fast
To *Pans* imbraces, with the haste
Shee fled him once, whose reede-pipe rent
He finds now a *new Instrument*.
Theseus return'd, invokes the Ayre
And windes, then wafts his faire;
Whilst *Ariadne* ravish't stood
Halfe in his armes, halfe in the flood.

Proud *Anaxarete* doth fall
At *Iphis* feete, who smiles of all:
And he (whilst she his curles doth deck)
Hangs no where now, but on her neck.
    Here *Phœbus* with a beame untombes
    Long-hid *Leucothoë*, and dombes
Her father there; *Daphne* the faire
Knowes now no bayes but round her haire;
And to *Apollo* and his Sons
Who pay him their due Orisons,
Bequeaths her Lawrell-robe, that flame
Contemnes, Thunder and evill Fame.

There kneel'd *Adonis* fresh as spring,
Gaye as his youth, now offering
Her selfe those joyes with voice and hand,
Which first he could not understand.

Transfixed *Venus* stood amas'd,
Full of the Boye and Love, she gaz'd
And in imbraces seemed more
Sencelesse and colde, then he before.
Uselesse Childe! In vaine (said she)
You beare that fond Artillerie:
See heere a Pow'r above the slow
Weake execution of thy bow.

So said, she riv'd the Wood in two,
Unedged all his Arrowes too,
And with the string their feathers bound
To that part whence we have our wound.

See, see! the darts by which we burn'd
Are bright *Löysa's* pencills turn'd;
With which she now enliveth more
Beauties, than they destroy'd before.

An Elegie.

Princesse KATHERINE *borne, christened, buried in one day.*

You, that can aptly mix your joyes with cries,
And weave white Iös with black Elegies,
Can Caroll out a Dirge, and in one breath
Sing to the Tune, either of life, or death;
You, that can weepe the gladnesse of the spheres,
And pen a Hymne in stead of Inke with teares,
Here, here, your unproportion'd wit let fall

To celebrate this new-borne Funerall,
And greete that little Greatnesse, which from th' wombe
Dropt both a load to th' Cradle, and the Tombe.

Bright soule! teach us to warble, with what feet
Thy swathing linnen, and thy winding sheet,
Mourne or shout forth that Fonts solemnitie,
Which at once buried, and christ'ned thee,
And change our shriller passions with that sound,
First told thee into th' ayre, then the ground.

   Ah wert thou borne for this, only to call
The *King* and *Queen* guests to your buriall?
To bid good night, your day not yet begun,
And showe's a setting, ere a rising Sun?

   Or wouldst thou have thy life a Martyrdom?
Dye in the Act of thy Religion;
Fit, excellently, innocently good,
First sealing it with water, then thy blood?
As when on blazing wings a blest man sores,
And having past to God through fiery dores
Straight's roab'd with flames, when the same Element,
Which was his shame, proves now his Ornament;

   Oh how he hast'ned death, burn't to be fryed,
Kill'd twice with each delay, 'till deified:
So swift hath been thy race, so full of flight,
Like him condemn'd, ev'n aged with a night,
Cutting all lets with clouds, as if th' hadst been
Angels plum'd, and borne a *Cherubin*.

   Or in your journey towards Heav'n, say,
Tooke you the World a little in your way?
Saw'st and dislik'st its vaine pompe then didst flye
Up for eternall glories to the skye?
Like a Religious Ambitious one
Aspiredst for the everlasting Crowne?

Ah holy Traytour to your brother Prince,
Rob'd of his birth-right and preheminence:
Could you ascend yon' Chaire of State e're him,
And snatch from th' heire the Starry Diadem?
Making your honours now as much uneven,
As Gods on earth, are lesse then Saints in Heav'n.

Triumph! sing triumphs, then! Oh put on all
Your richest lookes drest for this Festivall;
Thoughts full of ravisht reverence, with eyes
So fixt as when a Saint we canonize;
Clap wings with *Seraphins* before the Throne
At this eternall Coronation,
And teach your soules new mirth, such as may be
Worthy this Birth-day to Divinity.

But ah! these blast your feasts, the Jubilies
We send you up are sad, as were our cries,
And of true joy, we can expresse no more
Thus crown'd, then when we buried thee before.

Princesse in heav'n forgivenes! whilst we
Resigne our office to the *Hierarchy*.

Love Conquer'd
A Song
Set by Mr. *Henry Lawes*.

I

The childish God of Love did sweare
    Thus: by my awfull Bow and Quiver,
Yon' weeping, kissing, smiling pair,
    I'le scatter all their vowes i' th' Ayr,
And their knit imbraces shiver.

II

Up then to th' head with his best Art,
    Full of spite and envy blowne,
At her constant Marble Heart,
    He drawes his swiftest surest dart,
Which bounded back, and hit his owne.

III

Now the Prince of fires burnes!
    Flames in the luster of her eyes;
Triumphant she, refuses, scornes;
    He submits, adores, and mournes,
And is his Votresse Sacrifice.

IV

Foolish Boye! Resolve me now
    What 'tis to sigh and not be heard?
He weeping, kneel'd, and made a vow,
    The world shall love as yon' fast two,
So on his sing'd wings up he steer'd.

A loose SARABAND
Set by Mr. *Henry Lawes*

I

Ah me! the little Tyrant Theefe!
    As once my heart was playing,
He snatcht it up and flew away,
    Laughing at all my praying.

II

Proud of his purchase he surveyes,
    And curiously sounds it,
And though he sees it full of wounds,
    Cruel still on he wounds it.

III

And now this heart is all his sport,
    Which as a Ball he boundeth
From hand to breast, from breast to lip,
    And all it's rest confoundeth.

IV

Then as a Top he sets it up,
    And pitifully whips it;
Sometimes he cloathes it gay and fine,
    Then straight againe he strips it.

V

He cover'd it with *false beliefe*,
    Which gloriously show'd it;
And for a morning-Cushionet
    On's Mother he bestow'd it.

VI

Each day with her small brazen stings,
    A thousand times she rac'd it;
But then at night, bright with her Gemmes,
    Once neere her breast she plac'd it.

VII

There warme it gan to throb and bleed;
    She knew that smart and grieved;
At length this poore condemned Heart
    With these rich drugges repreeved.

VIII

She washt the wound with a fresh teare,
    Which my *Lucasta* dropped,
And in the sleave-silke of her haire,
    'Twas hard bound up and wrapped.

IX

She proab'd it with her constancie,
    And found no Rancor nigh it;
Only the anger of her eye,
    Had wrought some proud flesh by it.

X

Then prest she *Narde* in ev'ry veine
    Which from her kisses trilled;
And with the balme heald all its paine
    That from her hand distilled.

XI

But yet this heart avoyds me still,
    Will not by me be owned;
But's fled to it's *Physitians* breast,
    There proudly sits inthroned.

A forsaken Lady to her false Servant that is disdained by his new Mistris

Were it that you so shun me 'cause you wish
    (Cruels't) a fellow in your wretchednesse,
Or that you take some small ease in your owne
Torments, to heare another sadly groane,
I were most happy in my paines, to be
So truely blest, to be so curst by thee:
But Oh! my cries to that doe rather adde,
Of which too much already thou hast had,
And thou art gladly sad to heare my moane;
Yet sadly hearst me with derision.

    Thou most unjust, that really dost know,
        And feelst thy selfe the flames I burne in, Oh!
How can you beg to be set loose from that
Consuming stake, you binde another at?

Uncharitablest both wayes, to denie
That pity me, for which your selfe must dye,
To love not her loves you, yet know the paine
What 'tis to love, and not be lov'd againe.

Flye on, flye on swift Racer, untill she
Whom thou of all ador'st shall learne of thee,
The pace t' outfly thee, and shall teach thee groan,
What terrour 'tis t' outgo, and be outgon.

Not yet looke back, nor yet, must we
Run then like spoakes in wheeles eternally
And never overtake? Be dragg'd on still
By the weake Cordage of your untwin'd will,
Round without hope of rest? No, I will turne
And with my goodnes boldly meete your scorne;
My goodnesse which Heav'n pardon, and that fate
Made you hate love, and fall in love with hate.

But I am chang'd! bright reason that did give
My soule a noble quicknes, made me live
One breath yet longer, and to will, and see,
Hath reacht me pow'r to scorne as well as thee:
That thou which proudly tramplest on my grave,
Thy selfe mightst fall, conquer'd my double slave,
That thou mightst sinking in thy triumphs moan,
And I triumph in my destruction.

Hayle holy cold! chaste temper hayle! the fire
Rav'd o're my purer thoughts I feel t' expire,
And I am candied Ice; yee pow'rs! If e're
I shall be forc't unto my Sepulcher;
Or violently hurl'd into my Urne,
Oh make me choose rather to freeze, then burne.

Orpheus *to* Beasts
Song
Set by Mr. Curtes

I.
Here, here, oh here *Euridice,*
 Here was she slaine;
Her soule 'still'd through a veine:
 The Gods knew lesse
That time Divinitie,
 Then ev'n, ev'n these
 Of brutishnesse.

II.
Oh could you view the Melodie
 Of ev'ry grace,
And Musick of her face,
 You'd drop a teare,
Seeing more Harmonie
 In her bright eye,
 Then now you heare.

Orpheus *to* Woods
Song
Set by Mr. Curtes

Heark! Oh heark! you guilty Trees,
In whose gloomy Galleries
Was the cruell'st murder done,
That e're yet eclipst the Sunne;
Be then henceforth in your twigges
Blasted e're you sprout to sprigges;
Feele no season of the yeere,
But what shaves off all your haire,
Nor carve any from your wombes
Ought but Coffins, and their Tombes

The Grasse-hopper
To my Noble Friend, Mr.
Charles Cotton
Ode

I

Oh thou that swing'st upon the waving haire
    Of some well-filled Oaten Beard,
Drunke ev'ry night with a Delicious teare
    Dropt thee from Heav'n, where now th'art reard.

II

The Joyes of Earth and Ayre are thine intire,
    That with thy feet and wings dost hop and flye;
And when thy Poppy workes thou dost retire
    To thy Carv'd Acorn-bed to lye.

III

Up with the day, the Sun thou welcomst then,
    Sportst in the guilt-plats of his Beames,
And all these merry dayes mak'st merry men,
    Thy selfe, and Melancholy streames.

IV

But ah the Sickle! Golden Eares are Cropt;
    Ceres and *Bacchus* bid good-night;
Sharpe frosty fingers all your Flowr's have topt,
    And what sithes spar'd, Winds shave off quite.

V

Poore verdant foole! and now green Ice, thy Joys
    Large and as lasting, as thy Peirch of Grasse,
Bid us lay in 'gainst Winter, Raine, and poize
    Their flouds, with an o'erflowing glasse.

VI

Thou best of *Men* and *Friends*! we will create
    A Genuine Summer in each others breast;
And spite of this cold Time and frosen Fate
    Thaw us a warme seate to our rest.

VII

Our sacred harthes shall burne eternally
    As Vestall Flames, the North-wind, he
Shall strike his frost-stretch'd Winges, dissolve and flye
    This *Ætna* in Epitome.

VIII

Dropping *December* shall come weeping in,
    Bewayle th' usurping of his Raigne;
But when in show'rs of old Greeke we beginne,
    Shall crie, he hath his Crowne againe!

IX

Night as cleare *Hesper* shall our Tapers whip
    From the light Casements, where we play,
And the darke Hagge from her black mantle strip,
    And sticke there everlasting Day.

X

Thus richer then untempted Kings are we,
    That asking nothing, nothing need:
Though Lord of all what Seas imbrace; yet he
    That wants himselfe, is poore indeed.

Dialogue

Lucasta, Alexis.
Set by Mr. *John Gamble*

I
Lucasta
Tell me *Alexis* what this parting is,
    That so like dying is, but is not it?

Alexis
It is a *swounding* for a while from blisse,
    'Till kind *how doe you* call's us from the fit.
If then the spirits only stray, let mine
Fly to thy bosome.

Lucasta
And my Soule to thine.

Chorus
Thus in our native seate we gladly give
Our right, for one where we can better live.

II
Lucasta
But Ah this ling'ring murdring Farewel!
Death quickly wounds, & wounding cures the ill.

Alexis
It is the glory of a valiant Lover,
Still to be dying, still for to recover.

Chorus
Soldiers suspected of their courage goe,
That Ensignes, and their Breasts untorne show:
Love nee're his Standard when his Hoste he sets,
Creates alone fresh-bleeding *Bannerets*.

III
Alexis
But part we, when thy Figure I retaine
    Still in my Heart, still strongly in mine Eye?

Lucasta
Shadowes no longer than the Sun remaine,
    But when his beams that made 'em fly, they fly.

Chorus
Vaine dreames of Love! that only so much blisse
Allow us, as to know our wretchednesse;
And deale a larger measure in our Paine
By showing Joy, then hiding it againe.

IV
Alexis
No, whilst light raigns, *Lucasta* still rules here,
And all the night shines wholy in this sphere:

Lucasta
I know no Morne but my *Alexis* Ray,
To my dark thoughts the breaking of the day.

Chorus
Alexis
So in each other if the pitying Sun
Thus keep us fixt; nere may his Course be run!

Lucasta
And Oh! if Night us undivided make;
Let us sleepe still, and sleeping never wake!

The Close
Cruel *Adieu's* may well adjourne awhile
The Sessions of a Looke, a Kisse, or Smile,
And leave behinde an angry grieving Blush;
But time nor Fate can part us joyned thus.

To Ellinda,
That lately I have not written

I

If in me Anger, or disdaine
In you, or both, made me refraine
From th' Noble intercourse of Verse,
That only Vertuous thoughts rehearse;
    Then Chaste *Ellinda* might you feare
    The sacred Vowes that I did sweare.

II

But if alone some pious thought
Me to an inward sadnesse brought,
Thinking to breath your Soule too well,
My tongue was charmed with that spell;
    And left it (since there was no roome
    To Voyce your worth enough) strooke dumbe.

III

So then this *Silence* doth reveale
No thought of Negligence, but Zeale:
For as in Adoration,
This is Loves true Devotion:
    Children and Fooles the words repeate,
    But *Anch'rites* pray in teares and sweate.

Sonnet
Set by Mr. *William Lawes*

I

When I by thy faire shape did sweare,
    And mingled with each Vowe a teare,
      I lov'd, I lov'd thee best,
      I swore as I profest;

For all the while you lasted warme and pure,
  My Oathes too did endure;
But once turn'd faithlesse to thy selfe, and Old,
They then with thee incessantly grew Cold.

II

I swore my selfe thy Sacrifice
By th' *Ebon* Bowes that guard thine eyes,
  Which now are alter'd White,
  And by the glorious Light
Of both those Stars, of which their Spheres bereft
  Only the Gellie's left:
Then changed thus, no more I'm bound to you
Then swearing to a Saint that proves untrue.

Lucasta *Weeping*
Song. Set by Mr. *John Laneere*

I

Lucasta wept, and still the bright
  Inamour'd God of Day,
With his soft Handkercher of Light,
  Kist the wet Pearles away.

II

But when her Teares his heate or'e came,
  In Cloudes he quensht his Beames,
And griev'd, wept out his Eye of Flame,
  So drowned her sad Streames.

III

At this she smil'd, when straight the Sun
  Cleer'd, with her kinde desires;
And by her eyes Reflection,
  Kindled againe his Fires.

The Vintage *to the* Dungeon. A Song
Set by Mr. *William Lawes*

I.

Sing out pent Soules, sing cheerefully!
Care Shackles you in Liberty,
Mirth frees you in Captivity:
    Would you double fetters adde?
    Else why so sadde?

Chorus
Besides your pinion'd armes you'l finde
Griefe too can manakell the minde.

II.

Live then Pris'ners uncontrol'd;
Drink oth' strong, the Rich, the Old,
Till Wine too hath your Wits in hold;
    Then if still your Jollitie,
    And Throats are free;

Chorus
Tryumph in your Bonds and Paines,
And daunce to th' Musick of your Chaines.

On the Death of Mrs. ELIZABETH FILMER
An Elegiacall Epitaph

I

You that shall live awhile before
Old Time tyr's, and is no more;
When that this Ambitious Stone
Stoopes low as what it tramples on;
Know that in that Age when Sinne

Gave the World Law, and governd Queene,
A Virgin liv'd, that still put on
White Thoughts, though out of fashion;
That trac't the Stars, 'spite of report,
And durst be good, though chidden for't:
Of Such a Soule that Infant Heav'n
Repented what it thus had giv'n;
For finding equall happy man,
Th' impatient Pow'rs snatch it agen:
Thus Chaste as th' Ayre whither shee's fled,
She making her Celestiall bed
In her warme Alablaster lay
As cold is in this house of Clay;
Nor were the Rooms unfit to feast
Or Circumscribe This Angel-guest;
The Radiant Gemme was brightly set
In as Divine a Carkanet;
For which the clearer was not knowne,
Her Minde, or her Complexion:
Such an everlasting Grace,
Such a beatifick Face
Incloysters here this narrow floore
That possest all hearts before.
    Blest and bewayl'd in Death and Birth!
The smiles and teares of Heav'n and Earth!
Virgins at each step are afeard,
FILMER is shot by which they steer'd,
Their Star extinct, their beauty dead
That the yong world to honour led;
But see! the rapid Spheres stand still,
And tune themselves unto her will.
    Thus, although this Marble must,
As all things crumble into dust,
And though you finde this faire-built Tombe
Ashes, as what lyes in it's Wombe;
Yet her Saint-like name shall shine
A living Glory to this Shrine,

And her eternall Fame be read,
When all, but *very Vertue's dead*.

To Lucasta. *From Prison*
An Epode

I

Long in thy Shackels, liberty,
   I ask not from these walls, but thee;
Left for a while anothers Bride,
To fancy all the world beside.

II

   Yet e're I do begin to love,
See! How I all my objects prove;
     Then my free Soule to that confine,
     'Twere possible I might call mine.

III

First I would be in love with *Peace*,
   And her rich swelling breasts increase;
But how alas! how may that be,
   Despising Earth, she will love me?

IV

Faine would I be in love with *War*,
   As my deare Just avenging star;
But War is loved so ev'ry where,
   Ev'n He disdaines a Lodging here.

V

Thee and thy wounds I would bemoane
   Faire thorough-shot *Religion*;
But he lives only that kills thee,
   And who so bindes thy hands, is free.

VI

I would love a *Parliament*
   As a maine Prop from Heav'n sent;
But ah! Who's he that would be wedded
   To th' fairest body that's beheaded?

VII

Next would I court my *Liberty*,
   And then my Birth-right, *Property*;
But can that be, when it is knowne
   There's nothing you can call your owne?

VIII

A *Reformation* I would have,
   As for our griefes a *Sov'raigne* salve;
That is, a cleansing of each wheele
   Of State, that yet some rust doth feele:

IX

But not a Reformation so,
   As to reforme were to ore'throw;
Like Watches by unskilfull men
   Disjoynted, and set ill againe.

X

The *Publick Faith* I would adore,
   But she is banke-rupt of her store;
Nor how to trust her can I see,
   For she that couzens all, must me.

XI

Since then none of these can be
   Fit objects for my Love and me;
What then remaines, but th' only spring
   Of all our loves and joyes? The KING.

XII

He who being the whole Ball
   Of Day on Earth, lends it to all;
When seeking to ecclipse his right,
   Blinded, we stand in our owne light.

XIII

And now an universall mist
   Of Error is spread or'e each breast,
With such a fury edg'd, as is
   Not found in th' inwards of th' Abysse.

XIV

Oh from thy glorious Starry Waine
   Dispense on me one sacred Beame
To light me where I soone may see
   How to serve you, and you trust me.

Lucasta's Fanne,
With a Looking glasse in it

I

Eastrich! Thou featherd Foole, and easie prey,
   That larger sailes to thy broad Vessell needst;
Snakes through thy guttur-neck hisse all the day,
   Then on thy I'ron Messe at supper feedst.

II

Oh what a glorious transmigration
   From this, to so divine an edifice
Hast thou straight made! neere from a winged stone
   Transform'd into a Bird of Paradice!

III

Now doe thy Plumes for hiew and Luster vie
    With th' Arch of heav'n that triumphs or'e past wet,
And in a rich enamel'd pinion lye
    With Saphyres, Amethists, and Opalls set.

IV

Sometime they wing her side, then strive to drown
    The Day's eyes piercing beames, whose am'rous heat
Sollicites still, 'till with this shield of down
    From her brave face, his glowing fires are beat.

V

But whilst a plumy curtaine she doth draw,
    A Chrystall Mirror sparkles in thy breast,
In which her fresh aspect when as she saw,
    And then her Foe retired to the West.

VI

Deare *Engine* that oth' Sun got'st me the day,
    'Spite of his hot assaults mad'st him retreat!
No wind (said she) dare with thee henceforth play
    But mine own breath to coole the Tyrants heat.

VII

My lively shade thou ever shalt retaine
    In thy inclosed feather-framed glasse,
And but unto our selves to all remaine
    Invisible thou feature of this face!

VIII

So said, her sad Swaine over-heard, and cried
    Yee Gods! for faith unstain'd this a reward!
Feathers and glasse t'outweigh my vertue tryed?
    Ah show their empty strength! the Gods accord.

IX
Now fall'n the brittle Favourite lyes, and burst!
   Amas'd *Lucasta* weepes, repents, and flies
To her *Alexis*, vowes her selfe acurst
   If hence she dresse her selfe, but in his eyes.

LUCASTA, *taking the waters at Tunbridge*

Ode

I
Yee happy floods! that now must passe
   The sacred conduicts of her Wombe,
Smooth, and transparent as your face,
   When you are deafe, and windes are dumbe.

II
Be proud! and if your Waters be
   Foul'd with a counterfeyted teare,
Or some false sigh hath stained yee,
   Haste, and be purified there.

III
And when her Rosie gates y' have trac'd,
   Continue yet some Orient wet,
'Till turn'd into a Gemme, y'are plac'd
   Like Diamonds with Rubies set.

IV
Yee drops that dew th' *Arabian* bowers
   Tell me did you e're smell or view
On any leafe of all your flowers
   Soe sweet a sent, so rich a hiew?

V

But as through th' Organs of her breath,
    You trickle wantonly, beware;
Ambitious Seas in their just death
    As well as Lovers must have share.

VI

And see! you boyle as well as I,
    You that to coole her did aspire,
Now troubled, and neglected lye,
    Nor can your selves quench your owne fire.

VII

Yet still be happy in the thought,
    That in so small a time as this,
Through all the *Heavens* you were brought
    Of *Vertue, Honour, Love* and *Blisse.*

To Lucasta
Ode *Lyrick*

I

Ah *Lucasta*, why so Bright!
Spread with early streaked light!
If still vailed from our sight,
What is't but eternall night?

II

Ah *Lucasta*, why so Chaste?
With that vigour, ripenes grac't!
Not to be by Man imbrac't
Makes that Royall coyne imbace't,
And this golden Orchard waste.

III

Ah *Lucasta*, why so Great!
That thy crammed coffers sweat;
Yet not owner of a seat
May shelter you from Natures heat,
And your earthly joyes compleat.

IV

Ah *Lucasta*, why so Good!
Blest with an unstained flood
Flowing both through soule and blood;
If it be not understood,
'Tis a Diamond in mud.

V

Lucasta! stay! why dost thou flye?
Thou art not Bright, but to the eye,
Nor Chaste, but in the Mariage-tye,
Nor Great, but in this Treasurie,
Nor Good, but in that sanctitie.

VI

Harder then the Orient stone,
Like an Apparition,
Or as a pale shadow gone
Dumbe and deafe she hence is flowne.

VII

Then receive this equall dombe,
Virgins strow no teare or bloome,
No one dig the *Parian* wombe;
Raise her marble heart ith' roome,
And 'tis both her Coarse and Tombe.

To my Worthy Friend Mr.
Peter Lilly : *on that excellent Picture*
of his Majesty, and the Duke
of Yorke, drawne by him
at Hampton-Court

See! what a *clouded Majesty!* and eyes
Whose glory through their mist doth brighter rise!
See! what an humble bravery doth shine,
And griefe triumphant breaking through each line;
How it commands the face! so sweet a scorne
Never did *happy misery* adorne!
So sacred a contempt, that others show
To this, (oth' height of all the wheele) below;
That mightiest Monarchs by this shaded booke
May coppy out their proudest, richest looke.

   Whilst the true *Eaglet* this quick luster spies,
And by his *Sun's* enlightens his owne eyes;
He cares his cares, his burthen feeles, then streight
Joyes that so lightly he can beare such weight;
Whilst either eithers passion doth borrow,
And both doe grieve the same victorious sorrow.

   These, my best *Lilly* with so bold a spirit
And soft a grace, as if thou didst inherit
For that time all their greatnesse, and didst draw
With those brave eyes your *Royal Sitters* saw.

   Not as of old, when a rough hand did speake
A strong Aspect, and a faire face, a weake;
When only a black beard cried Villaine, and
By *Hieroglyphicks* we could understand;
When Chrystall typified in a white spot,
And the bright Ruby was but one red blot;
Thou dost the things *Orientally* the same,
Not only paintst its colour, but its *Flame*:

Thou sorrow canst designe without a teare,
And with the Man his very *Hope or Feare*;
So that th' amazed world shall henceforth finde
None but my *Lilly* ever drew a *Minde*.

Elinda's Glove

Sonnet

I

Thou snowy Farme with thy five Tenements!
    Tell thy white Mistris here was one
      That call'd to pay his dayly Rents:
But she agathering Flowr's and Hearts is gone,
And thou left voyd to rude Possession.

II

But grieve not pretty *Ermin* Cabinet,
    Thy Alablaster Lady will come home;
      If not, what Tenant can there fit
The slender turnings of thy narrow Roome,
But must ejected be by his owne dombe?

III

Then give me leave to leave my Rent with thee;
    Five kisses, one unto a place:
      For though the *Lute's* too high for me;
Yet Servants knowing Minikin nor Base,
Are still allow'd to fiddle with the Case.

To Fletcher reviv'd

How have I bin Religious? what strange good
Ha's scap't me that I never understood?
Have I Hel-guarded *Hæresie* o'rthrowne?
Heald wounded States? made Kings and Kingdoms one?
That *Fate* should be so merciful to me,
To let me live t' have said I have read thee.

  Faire Star ascend! the Joy! the Life! the Light
Of this tempestuous Age, this darke worlds sight!
Oh from thy Crowne of Glory dart one flame
May strike a sacred Reverence, whilest thy Name
(Like holy *Flamens* to their God of Day)
We bowing, sing; and whilst we praise, we pray.

  Bright Spirit! whose Æternal motion
Of Wit, like *Time*, stil in it selfe did run,
Binding all others in it, and did give
Commission, how far this or that shal live;
Like *Destiny* of Poems, who, as she
Signes death to all, her selfe can never dye.

  And now thy purple-robed *Tragaedy*,
In her imbroider'd Buskins, cals mine eye,
Where the brave *Aëtius* we see betray'd,
T' obey his Death, whom thousand lives obey'd;
Whilst that the *Mighty Foole* his Scepter breakes,
And through his *Gen'rals* wounds his own doome speakes,
Weaving thus richly *Valentinian*
The costliest Monarch with the cheapest man.

  Souldiers may here to their old glories adde,
The *Lover* love, and be with reason *mad*:
Not, as of old, *Alcides* furious,
Who wilder then his Bull did teare the house,
(Hurling his Language with the Canvas stone)
Twas thought the Monster ror'd the sob'rer Tone.

But ah! when thou thy sorrow didst inspire
With Passions, Blacke as is her darke attire,
Virgins as *Sufferers* have wept to see
So white a Soule, so red a Crueltie;
That thou hast griev'd, and with unthought redresse,
Dri'd their wet eyes who now thy mercy blesse;
Yet loth to lose thy watry jewell, when
Joy wip't it off, Laughter straight sprung't agen.

Now ruddy cheeked *Mirth* with Rosie wings,
Fans ev'ry brow with gladnesse, whilst she sings
Delight to all, and the whole Theatre
A Festivall in Heaven doth appeare:
Nothing but Pleasure, Love, and (like the Morne)
Each face a gen'ral smiling doth adorne.

Heare ye foul Speakers, that pronounce the Aire
Of Stewes and Shores, I will informe you where
And how to cloath aright your wanton wit,
Without her nasty Bawd attending it:
View here a loose thought sayd with such a grace,
Minerva might have spoke in *Venus* face;
So well disguis'd, that 'twas conceiv'd by none
But *Cupid* had *Diana's* linnen on;

And all his naked parts so vail'd, th' expresse
The shape with clowding the uncomlinesse;
That if this *Reformation*, which we
Receiv'd, had not been buried with thee,
The Stage (as this worke) might have liv'd and lov'd
Her Lines, the austere *Skarlet* had approv'd;
And th' *Actors* wisely been from that offence
As cleare, as they are now from *Audience*.

Thus with thy *Genius* did the *Scæne* expire,
Wanting thy Active and correcting fire,
That now (to spread a darknesse over all)

Nothing remaines but *Poesie* to fall:
And though from these thy *Embers* we receive
Some warmth, so much as may be said, we live,
That we dare praise thee, blushlesse, in the head
Of the best piece *Hermes* to *Love* e're read;
That We rejoyce and glory in thy Wit,
And feast each other with remembring it,
That we dare speak thy thought, thy Acts recite;
Yet all men henceforth be afraid to write.

The Lady *A. L.*
My Asylum *in a great extremity*

With that delight the Royal Captiv's brought
Before the Throne, to breath his farewell thought,
To tel his last tale, and so end with it;
Which gladly he esteemes a Benefit;
When the brave Victor at his great Soule dumbe
Findes something there, Fate cannot overcome,
Cals the chain'd Prince, and by his glory led,
First reaches him his Crowne, and then his Head;
Who ne're 'til now thinks himself slave and poor;
For though nought else, he had himselfe before;
He weepes at this faire chance, nor wil allow,
But that the Diadem doth brand his brow,
And under-rates himselfe below mankinde,
Who first had lost his Body, now his Minde.

 With such a Joy came I to heare my Dombe,
And haste the preparation of my Tombe,
When like good Angels who have heav'nly charge
To steere and guide mans sudden giddy barge,
She snatcht me from the Rock I was upon,
And landed me at lifes Pavillion:
Where I thus wound out of th' immense Abysse,
Was straight set on a Pinacle of Blisse.

    Let me leape in againe! and by that Fall
Bring me to my first woe, so cancel all:
Ah's this a quitting of the debt you owe,
To Crush her and her goodnesse at one blowe?
    Defend me from so foule Impiety,
Would make Friends grieve, & Furies weep to see.

    Now ye Sage Spirits which infuse in Men
That are oblidg'd, twice to oblige agen;
Informe my tongue in Labour, what to say,
And in what Coyne or Language to repay;
But you are silent as the Ev'nings Ayre,
When windes unto their hollow Grots repair:
    Oh then accept the all that left me is,
Devout Oblations of a sacred Wish!

    When she walks forth, ye perfum'd wings oth' East
Fan her, 'til with the Sun she hastes to th' West,
And when her heav'nly course calles up the day,
And breakes as bright, descend some glistering ray,
To Circle her, and her as glistering Haire,
That all may say a living Saint shines there;
Slow Time with woollen feet make thy soft pace,
And leave no tracks ith' snow of her pure face:
But when this Vertue must needs fall, to rise,
The brightest constellation in the Skies,
When we in Characters of Fire shall reade
How Cleere she was alive, how spotles Dead;
All you that are a kinne to Piety,
For onely you can her close mourners be,
Draw neer, and make of hallowed teares a Dearth
Goodnes and Justice both, are fled the Earth.

    If this be to be thankful, I'v a Heart
Broaken with Vowes, eaten with grateful smart,
And beside this, the Vild World nothing hath
Worth any thing, but her provoked Wrath:

So then who thinkes to satisfie in time,
Must give a satisfaction for that Crime:
Since she alone knowes the Gifts value, She
Can onely to her selfe requitall be,
And worthyly to th' Life paynt her owne Story
In it's true Colours and full native Glory;
Which when perhaps she shal be heard to tell,
Buffoones and Theeves ceasing to do ill,
Shal blush into a Virgin-Innocence,
And then woo others from the same offence;
The Robber and the Murderer in 'spite
Of his red spots shal startle into White:
All good (Rewards layd by) shal stil increase
For Love of her, and Villany decease;
Naught be ignote, not so much out of Feare
Of being punisht, as offending Her:

   So that when as my future daring Bayes
Shall bow it selfe in Lawrels to her praise,
To Crown her Conqu'ring Goodnes & proclaime
The due renowne, and Glories of her Name;
My Wit shal be so wretched, and so poore,
That 'stead of praysing I shal scandal her,
And leave when with my purest Art I'v done
Scarce the Designe of what she is begunne;
Yet men shal send me home, admir'd, exact,
Proud that I could from Her so wel detract.

   Where then thou bold Instinct shal I begin
My endlesse taske? To thanke her were a sin
Great as not speake, and not to speake a blame
Beyond what's worst, such as doth want a Name;
So thou my All, poore Gratitude, ev'n thou
In this, wilt an unthankful Office do:
Or wilt I fling all at her feet I have?
My Life, my Love, my very Soule a Slave?
Tye my free Spirit onely unto her,

And yeeld up my Affection Prisoner?
Fond Thought in this thou teachest me to give
What first was hers, since by her breath I live;
And hast but show'd me how I may resigne
Possession of those thing are none of mine.

A *Prologue* to the Scholars
A Comædy *presented at the White Fryers*

A Gentleman to give us somewhat new,
Hath brought up *Oxford* with him to show you;
Pray be not frighted – Tho the Scæne and Gown's
The *Universities*, the Wit's the Town's;
The Lines each honest *Englishman* may speake;
Yet not mistake his Mother-tongue for *Greeke*,
For stil 'twas part of his vow'd Liturgie,
From learned Comedies *deliver me*!
Wishing all those that lov'd 'em here asleepe,
Promising *Scholars*, but no *Scholarship*.

You'd smile to see, how he do's vex and shake,
Speakes naught, but, if the *Prologue* do's but take,
Or the first Act were past the Pikes once, then—
Then hopes and Joys, then frowns and fears agen,
Then blushes like a Virgin now to be
Rob'd of his Comicall Virginity
In presence of you all; in short you'd say
More hopes of Mirth are in his looks then Play.

These feares are for the Noble and the Wise;
But if 'mongst you there are such fowle dead eyes
As can Damne unaraign'd, cal Law their Pow'rs,
Judging it sin enough that it is *Ours*,
And with the House shift their decreed Desires,
Faire still to th' *Blacke*, *Blacke* still to the *White-Fryers;*

He dos protest he wil sit down and weep
Castles and Pyramids ⎯⎯⎯⎯⎯⎯⎯
⎯⎯⎯⎯⎯⎯⎯⎯⎯⎯⎯ No, he wil on,
Proud to be rais'd by such *Destruction*,
So far from quarr'lling with himselfe and Wit,
That he wil thank them for the *Benefit*,
Since finding nothing worthy of their *Hate*,
They reach him that themselves must *Envy* at.

The Epilogue

The stubborne author of the trifle, Crime,
That just now cheated you of 2 hours' time,
Presumptuous, it lik't him, began to grow
Carelesse, whether it pleased you or no.

  But we who ground th' excellence of a Play
On what the women at the dores wil say,
Who judge it by the Benches, and afford
To take your money ere his Oath or word
His *Schollars* school'd, sayd if he had been wise
He should have wove in one, two *Comedies;*
The first for th' Gallery, in which the Throne
To their amazement should descend alone,
The rosin-lightning flash, and Monster spire
Squibs, and words hotter then his fire.

  Th' other for the Gentlemen oth' Pit,
Like to themselves, all Spirit, Fancy, Wit,
In which plots should be subtile as a Flame,
Disguises would make *Proteus* stil the same:
Humours so rarely humour'd, and exprest,
That ev'n they should thinke 'em so, not drest;
Vices acted and applauded too, Times
Tickled, and th' Actors acted, not their Crimes,

So he might equally applause have gain'd
Of th' hardned, sooty, and the snowy hand.

    Where now one *so so* spatters, t'other, no;
Tis his first Play, twere Solecisme 'tshould goe;
The next, 't shew'd pritily, but searcht within
It appeares bare and bald, as is his Chin;
The Towne-wit Sentences; a Scholars Play!
Pish! I know not why – but – th'ave not the way.

    We, whose gaine is all our pleasure, ev'n these
Are bound by Justice and Religion to please;
Which he whose Pleasure's all his gaine, goes by
As slightly, as they doe his Comædy.

    Cull's out the few the worthy, at whose feet
He sacrifices both himselfe, and it
His Fancies first fruits: Profit he knowes none
Unles that of your Approbation,
Which if your thoughts at going out will pay,
Hee'l not looke farther for a *Second Day*.

Clitophon *and* Lucippe *translated*

To the Ladies

Pray Ladies breath, awhile lay by
   Cælestial *Sydney's Arcady*;
Heere's a Story that doth Claime
A little respite from his Flame:
Then with a quick dissolving looke
Unfold the smoothnes of this book,
To which no Art (except your sight)
Can reach a worthy Epithite;
'Tis an Abstract of all Volumes

A Pillaster of all Columnes
Fancy e're rear'd to *Wit*, to be
The smallest Gods Epitome,
And so compactedly expresse
All Lovers pleasing Wretchednes.

    Gallant *Pamela's* Majesty
And her sweet Sisters Modesty
Are fixt in each of you; you are
Distinct, what these together were:
Divinest that are really
What *Cariclea's* feign'd to be;
That are ev'ry *one* the *Nine*,
And brighter here *Astrea's* shine,
View our *Lucippe*, and remaine
In her, these Beauties o're againe.

    Amazement! Noble *Clitophon*,
Ev'n now lookt somewhat colder on
His cooler Mistresse, and she too
Smil'd not as she us'd to do;
See! the Individuall Payre
Are at sad Oddes, and parted are;
They quarrell, æmulate, and stand
At strife, who first shal kisse your hand.

    A new Dispute there lately rose
Betwixt the *Greekes* and *Latines*, whose
Temple's should be bound with Glory
In best languaging this Story;
    Yee Heyres of Love, that with one *Smile*
    A ten-yeeres *War* can reconcile;
Peacefull *Hellens*! Vertuous! See!
The jarring Languages agree,
And here all Armes layd by, they doe
In English meet, to wayt on you.

To my truely valiant, learned Friend,
who in his booke resolv'd the Art Gladiatory into the Mathematick's

I
Hearke, Reader! wilt be learn'd ith' warres?
   A Gen'rall in a gowne?
Strike a league with Arts and Scarres,
   And snatch from each a Crowne?

II
Wouldst be a wonder? Such a one,
   As should win with a Looke?
A Bishop in a Garison,
   And Conquer by the Booke?

III
Take then this Mathematick shield,
   And henceforth by it's rules,
Be able to dispute ith' field,
   And Combate in the Schooles.

IV
Whilst peaceful Learning once againe,
   And the Souldier so concord,
As that he fights now with her Penne,
   And she writes with his Sword.

AMYNTOR'S GROVE
His Chloris, Arigo, *and* Gratiana

An Elogie

It was *Amyntor's* Grove, that *Chloris*
For ever Ecchoes and her Glories;

Chloris, the gentlest Sheapherdesse,
That ever Lawnes and Lambes did blesse;
Her Breath like to the whispering winde,
Was calme as thought, sweet as her Minde;
Her Lips like coral gates kept in
The perfume and the pearle within;
Her eyes a double-flaming torch
That alwayes shine, and never scorch:
Her selfe the Heav'n in which did meet
The *All* of bright, of faire and sweet.

   Here was I brought with that delight
That seperated Soules take flight;
And when my Reason call'd my sence
Back somewhat from this excellence,
That I could see; I did begin
T' observe the curious ordering
Of every Roome, where 'ts hard to know
Which most excels in *sent* or *show*:
Arabian gummes do breathe here forth,
And th' *East's* come over to the *North*;
The Windes have brought their hyre of sweet
To see *Amyntor Chloris* greet;
Balme and Nard, and each perfume,
To blesse this payre chafe and consume;
And th' *Phœnix*, see! already fries!
Her Neast a fire in *Chloris* eyes!

   Next the great and powerful hand
Beckens my thoughts unto a stand
Of *Titian, Raphael, Georgone*
Whose *Art* ev'n *Nature* hath out-done;
For if weake *Nature* only can
Intend, not perfect what is man,
These certainely we must prefer,
Who mended what *She* wrought, and *Her*;
And sure the shadowes of those rare

And kind incomparable fayre
Are livelier, nobler Company,
Then if they could or speake, or see:
For these I aske without a tush,
Can kisse or touch, without a blush,
And we are taught that *Substance* is,
If uninjoy'd, but th' shade of blisse.

   Now every Saint Cleerly divine,
Is clos'd so in her severall shrine;
The Gems so rarely, richly set,
For them wee love the Cabinet;
So intricately plac't withall,
As if th' imbrordered the Wall,
So that the Pictures seem'd to be
But one continued Tapistrie.

   After this travell of mine eyes
We sate, and pitied Dieties;
Wee bound our loose hayre with the Vine,
The Poppy, and the Eglantine;
One swell'd an Oriental bowle
Full, as a grateful, Loyal Soule
To *Chloris! Chloris!* heare, Oh heare!
'Tis pledg'd above in ev'ry Sphere.

   Now streight the *Indians* richest prize
Is kindled in glad Sacrifice;
Cloudes are sent up on wings of Thyme,
Amber, Pomgranates, Jessemine,
And through our Earthen Conduicts sore
Higher then Altars fum'd before.

   So drencht we our oppressing cares,
And choakt the wide Jawes of our feares,
Whilst ravisht thus we did devise,
If this were not a Paradice

In all, except these harmlesse sins;
Behold! flew in two *Cherubins*
Cleare as the skye from whence they came,
And brighter then the sacred Flame:
The Boy adorn'd with Modesty,
Yet armed so with Majesty;
That if the *Thunderer* againe
His Eagle sends, she stoops in vaine;
Besides his *Innocenc*e he tooke
A Sword and Casket, and did looke
Like *Love* in *Armes*; he wrote but five,
Yet spake eighteene, each *Grace* did strive,
And twenty *Cupids* thronged forth,
Who first should shew his prettier worth.

    But Oh the *Nymph!* did you ere know
Carnation mingled with *Snow*?
Or have you seene the Lightning shrowd,
And straight breake through th' opposing cloud?
So ran her blood such was its hue;
So through her vayle her bright Haire flew,
And yet its Glory did appeare
But thinne, because her *eyes* were neere.

    Blooming Boy, and blossoming Mayd,
May your faire Sprigges be neere betrayd
To eating worme or fouler storme;
No Serpent lurke to do them harme;
No sharpe frost cut, no North-winde teare,
The Verdure of that fragrant hayre;
But may the Sun and gentle weather,
When you are both growne ripe together,
Load you with fruit, such as your Father
From you with all the joyes doth gather:
And may you when one branch is dead
Graft such another in it's stead,
Lasting thus ever in your prime
'Till th' Sithe is snatcht away from *Time*.

Against the Love of Great Ones

Unhappy youth betrayd by Fate
To such a Love hath *Sainted Hate*,
And *damned* those *Cælestiall* bonds
Are onely knit with equal hands;
The Love of Great Ones? 'tis a Love
Gods are incapable to prove;
For where there is a Joy uneven,
There never, never can be Heav'n:
'Tis such a Love as is not sent
To Fiends as yet for punishment;
Ixion willingly doth feele
The Gyre of his eternal wheele,
Nor would he now exchange his paine
For Cloudes and Goddesses againe.

    Wouldst thou with tempests lye? Then bow
To th' rougher furrows of her brow,
Or make a Thunder-bolt thy Choyce?
Then catch at her more fatal Voyce;
Or 'gender with the Lightning? trye
The subtler Flashes of her eye:
Poore *Semele* wel knew the same,
Who both imbrac't her God and Flame;
And not alone in Soule did burne,
But in this Love did Ashes turne.

    How il doth Majesty injoy
The Bow and Gaity oth' Boy,
As if the *Purple-roabe* should sit,
And sentence give ith' Chayr of *Wit*.

    Say ever-dying wretch to whom
Each answer is a certaine dombe.
What is it that you would possesse,
The *Countes*, or the naked *Besse*?

Would you her *Gowne* or *Title* do?
Her *Box*, or *Gem*, her *Thing* or *show*?
If you meane *Her*, the very *Her*
Abstracted from her character;
Unhappy Boy! you may as soone
With fawning wanton with the Moone,
Or with an amorous Complaint
Get prostitute your very Saint;
Not that we are not mortal, or
Fly *Venus* Altars, or abhor
The selfesame Knack for which you pine;
But we (defend us!) are divine,
Female, but Madam borne, and come
From a right-honourable Wombe:
Shal we then mingle with the base,
And bring a silver-tinsell race?
Whilst th' issue Noble wil not passe,
The Gold allayd (almost halfe brasse)
And th' blood in each veine doth appeare,
Part thick *Booreinn*, part *Lady* Cleare:
Like to the sordid Insects sprung
From Father, *Sun*, and Mother *Dung*;
Yet lose we not the hold we have,
But faster graspe the trembling slave;
Play at Baloon with's heart, and winde
The strings like scaines, steale into his minde
Ten thousand *Hells* and *feigned Joyes*
Far worse then they, whilst like whipt Boys,
After this scourge hee's hush with Toys.

    This heard Sir, play stil in her eyes,
And be a dying, Lives, like Flyes
Caught by their Angle-legs, and whom
The Torch laughs peece-meale to consume.

Lucasta *paying her Obsequies to the Chast memory of my dearest Cosin* Mrs. Bowes Barne.

I

See! what an undisturbed teare
   She weepes for her last sleepe;
But, viewing her straight wak'd a *Star*,
   She weepes that she did weepe.

II

Griefe ne're before did Tyranize
   On th' Honour of that brow,
And at the wheeles of her brave Eyes
   Was Captive led til now.

III

Thus, for a Saints Apostacy
   The unimagin'd Woes
And sorrowes of the *Hierarchy*,
   None but an Angel knowes.

IV

Thus for lost soules Recovery,
   The Clapping of all Wings,
And Triumphs of this Victory,
   None but an Angel sings.

V

So none but *She* know's to bemone
   This equal Virgins Fate,
None but *Lucasta* can her Crowne
   Of Glory celebrate.

VI

Then dart on me (*Chast Light*) one ray
   By which I may discry

Thy Joy cleare through this cloudy Day
   To dresse my sorrow by.

To Althea,
From Prison
Song
Song Set by Dr. *John Wilson.*

I

When Love with unconfined wings
   Hovers within my Gates;
And my divine *Althea* brings
   To whisper at the Grates;
When I lye tangled in her haire
   And fettered to her eye;
The *Gods* that wanton in the Aire,
   Know no such Liberty.

II

When flowing Cups run swiftly round
   With no allaying *Thames*,
Our carelesse heads with Roses bound,
   Our hearts with Loyall Flames;
When thirsty griefe in Wine we steepe,
   When Healths and draughts go free,
Fishes that tipple in the Deepe,
   Know no such Libertie.

III

When (like committed linnets) I
   With shriller throat shall sing
The sweetnes, Mercy, Majesty,
   And glories of my King;
When I shall voyce aloud, how Good
   He is, how Great should be;
      Enlarged Winds that curle the Flood,
      Know no such Liberty.

IV

Stone Walls do not a Prison make,
   Nor I'ron bars a Cage;
Mindes innocent and quiet take
   That for an Hermitage;
If I have freedome in my Love,
   And in my soule am free;
Angels alone that sore above,
   Injoy such Liberty.

Being treated To Ellinda

For Cherries plenty, and for Coran's
   Enough for fifty, were there more on's;
For Elles of Beere Flutes of Canary
That well did wash downe pasties-mary;
For Peason, Chickens, sawces high,
Pig, and the Widdow-Venson pye;
With certaine promise (to your Brother)
Of the Virginity of another,
Where it is thought I too may peepe in
With Knuckles far as any deepe in;
For glasses, heads, hands, bellies full
Of Wine, and Loyne right-worshipfull;
Whether all of, or more behind-a
Thankes freest, freshest, Faire *Ellinda*:
Thankes for my Visit not disdaining,
Or at the least thankes for your feigning;
For if your mercy doore were lockt-well,
I should be justly soundly knockt-well;
Cause that in dogrell I did mutter
Not one Rhime to you from *dam-Rotter*.

   Next beg I to present my duty
To pregnant Sister in prime Beauty,

Whom well I deeme (e're few months elder)
Will take out *Hans* from pretty *Kelder*,
And to the sweetly fayre *Mabella*,
A match that vies with *Arabella;*
In each respect but the misfortune,
Fortune, Fate, I thee importune.

    Nor must I passe the lovely *Alice*,
Whose health I'd quaffe in golden Chalice;
But since that Fate hath made me neuter,
I only can in Beaker Pewter:
But who'd forget, or yet left un-sung
The doughty Acts of *George* the yong-Son?
Who yesterday to save his Sister
Had slaine the Snake, had he not mist her:
But I shall leave him 'till a Nag on
He gets to prosecute the Dragon;
And then with helpe of Sun and Taper,
Fill with his deeds twelve Reames of paper,
That *Amadis*, Sir *Guy*, and *Topaz*
With his fleet Neigher shall keep no-pace.
    But now to close all I must switch-hard.
    Servant ever;
               Lovelace Richard.

Sonnet
To Generall Goring,
after the pacification at Berwicke
A la Chabot

I

Now the *Peace* is made at the Foes rate,
Whilst men of Armes 'to Kettles their old Helmes translate,
    And drinke in Caskes of Honourable Plate;
        In ev'ry hand a Cup be found,

    That from all Hearts a health may sound
To *Goring*! to *Goring*! see't goe round.

II

    He whose Glories shine so brave and high,
That Captive they in Triumph leade each eare and eye,
      Claiming uncombated the Victorie,
        And from the Earth to Heav'n rebound
        Fixt there eternall as this Round
      To *Goring*! to *Goring*! see him Crown'd.

III

    To his lovely Bride in love with scars,
Whose eyes wound deepe in Peace, as doth his sword in wars;
      They shortly must depose the Queen of Stars:
        Her cheekes the Morning blushes give,
        And the benighted World repreeve,
      To *Lettice*! to *Lettice*! let her live.

IV

    Give me scorching heat, thy heat dry *Sun*,
That to this payre I may drinke off an Ocean
      Yet leave my grateful thirst unquensht, undone;
        Or a full Bowle of heav'nly wine,
        In which dissolved Stars should shine
      To the Couple! to the Couple! th' are Divine.

Sir Thomas Wortley's *Sonnet Answered*
The Sonnet

I

No more
  Thou little winged Archer, now no more
      As heretofore,
Thou maist pretend within my breast to bide,
      No more,

Since Cruell Death of dearest *Lyndamore*
                    Hath me depriv'd,
I bid adieu to Love, and all the world beside.

                    II
                    Go, go;
Lay by thy quiver and unbend thy Bow
                    Poore sillie Foe,
Thou spend'st thy shafts but at my breast in Vain,
                    Since Death
My heart hath with a fatall Icie Deart
                    Already slain,
Thou canst not ever hope to warme her wound,
          Or wound it o're againe.

The Answer

                    I

Againe,
Thou witty Cruell Wanton, now againe,
                    Through ev'ry Veine,
Hurle all your lightning, and strike ev'ry Dart.
                    Againe,
Before I feele this pleasing, pleasing paine,
          I have no Heart,
Nor can I live but sweetly murder'd with
          So deare, so deare a smart.

                    II
                    Then flye,
And kindle all your Torches at her Eye,
                    To make me Dye
Her Martyr, and put on my Roabe of Flame:
                    So I
Advanced on my blazing Wings on high,

       In Death became
Inthroan'd a Starre, and Ornament unto
         Her glorious glorious name.

A Guiltlesse Lady imprisoned: after penanced

Song
Set by Mr. *William Lawes*

Heark Faire one, how what e're here is
   Doth laugh and sing at thy distresse;
Not out of hate to thy reliefe,
   But Joy t' enjoy thee, though in griefe.

      II.
See! that which chaynes you, you chaine here;
   The Prison is thy Prisoner;
How much thy Jaylors Keeper art!
   He bindes your hands, but you his Heart.

      III.
The Gyves to Rase so smooth a skin,
   Are so unto themselves within,
But, blest to kisse so fayre an Arme
   Haste to be happy with that harme.

      IV.
And play about thy wanton wrist,
   As if in them thou so wert drest;
But if too rough, too hard they presse,
   Oh, they but Closely, closely kisse.

V.

And as thy bare feet blesse the Way
    The people doe not mock, but pray,
And call thee, as amas'd they run
    Instead of prostitute, a Nun.

VI.

The merry Torch burnes with desire
    To kindle the eternall Fire,
And lightly daunces in thine eyes
    To tunes of *Epithalamies*.

VII.

The sheet's ty'd ever to thy Wast,
    How thankfull to be so imbrac't!
And see! thy very very bands
    Are bound to thee, to binde such Hands.

Upon the Curtaine of Lucasta's *Picture, it was thus wrought*

Oh, stay that Covetous hand; first turn all Eye,
    All Depth and minde; then Mystically spye
Her Soul's faire Picture, her faire Soul's, in all
So truely Copied from th' Originall,
That you will sweare her body by this Law,
Is but its shadow, as this it's,—now draw.

To his Deare Brother Colonel F. L. *immoderately mourning my Brothers untimely Death at* Carmarthen

If Teares could wash the Ill away,
A Pearle for each wet bead I'd pay;
But as dew'd Corne the fuller growes,
So water'd eyes but swell our Woes.

II.
One drop another cals, which still
(Griefe adding Fuell) doth distill;
Too fruitfull of her selfe is Anguish,
We need no cherishing to Languish.

III.
Coward *Fate* degen'rate Man
Like little Children uses, when
He whips us first untill we weepe,
Then 'cause we still a weeping keepe.

IV.
Then from thy firme selfe never swerve;
Teares fat the Griefe that they should sterve;
I'ron decrees of Destinie
Are ner'e wipe't out with a wet Eye.

V.
But this way you may gaine the field,
Oppose but sorrow, and 'twill yield;
One gallant thorough-made Resolve
Doth *Starry Influence* dissolve.

An Elegie
On the Death of Mrs. Cassandra Cotton,
only Sister to Mr. C. Cotton.

Hither with hallowed steps as is the Ground
That must enshrine this Saint with lookes profound,
And sad aspects as the dark vails you weare
Virgins opprest, draw gently, gently neare;
Enter the dismall chancell of this roome,
Where each pale guest stands fixt a living Tombe,
With trembling hands helpe to remove this Earth
To its last death and first victorious birth:
Let Gums and incense fume, who are at strife
To enter th' Hearse and breath in it new life;
Mingle your steppes with flowers as you goe,
Which, as they haste to fade, will speake your woe.

And when y' have plac't your Tapers on her Urn,
How poor a tribute 'tis to weep and mourn!
That flood the channell of your Eye-lids fils,
When you lose trifles, or what's lesse, your Wills.
If you'l be worthy of these Obsequies,
Be blind unto the World, and drop your Eyes;
Waste and consume, burn downward as this fire
That's fed no more: so willingly expire;
Passe through the cold and obscure narrow way,
Then light your torches at the spring of Day,
There with her triumph in your Victory,
Such Joy alone and such Solemnity
Becomes this Funerall of Virginity.

Or, if you faint to be so blest: Oh heare!
If not to dye, dare but to live like her:
Dare to live Virgins, till the honour'd Age
Of thrice fifteen cals Matrons on the stage,
Whilst not a blemish or least staine is scene
On your white roabe 'twixt fifty and fifteene;

But as it in your swathing-bands was given,
Bring't in your winding sheet unsoyl'd to Heav'n.
Dare to do purely, without Compact good,
Or Herald, by no one understood
But him, who now in thanks bows either knee,
For th' early benefit and secresie.

    Dare to affect a serious holy sorrow,
To which Delights of Pallaces are narrow,
And, lasting as their smiles, dig you a roome,
Where practise the probation of your tombe;
With ever-bended knees and piercing Pray'r
Smooth the rough passe through craggy Earth to Ay'r;
Flame there as Lights that shipwrackt Mariners
May put in safely, and secure their feares,
Who, adding to your Joyes, now owe you theirs.

    Virgins, if thus you dare but Courage take
To follow her in Life, else through this Lake
Of Nature wade, and breake her earthly bars,
Y' are fixt with her upon a Throne of stars
Arched with a pure Heav'n Chrystaline,
Where round you Love and Joy for ever shine.

    But you are dumbe, as what you do lament,
More senseles then her very monument
Which at your weaknes weeps — Spare that vaine teare!
Enough to burst the rev'rend Sepulcher:
Rise and walk home; there groaning prostrate fall
And celebrate your owne sad Funerall;
For howsoe're you move, may heare or see,
You are more dead and buried then shee.

Lucasta's *World*
Epode

I.

Cold as the breath of winds that blow
To silver shot descending snow

    Lucasta sighed; when she did close
    The World in frosty chains!
    And then a frown to Rubies froze
        The blood boiled in our veins:

Yet cooled not the heat her Sphere
Of Beauties first had kindled there.

II.
Then moved, and with sudden Flame
Impatient to melt all againe,

    Straight from her eyes she lightning hurl'd,
        And Earth in ashes mournes;
    The Sun his blaze denies the world,
        And in her luster burns:

Yet warmed not the hearts, her nice
Disdaine had first congeal'd to Ice.

III
And now her teares nor griev'd desire
Can quench this raging, pleasing fire;

    Fate but one way allowes; behold
        Her smiles Divinity!
    They fanned this heat, and thaw'd that cold,
        So fram'd up a new sky.

Thus Earth from flames and Ice repreev'd,
E'er since hath in her Sun-shine liv'd.

To a Lady that desired me I would beare my part with her in a song Madam A. L.

This is the Prittiest Motion:
Madam, th' Alarums of a Drumme
That cals your Lord, set to your Cries,
To mine are sacred *Symphonies*.

    What, though 'tis said I have a Voice;
I know 'tis but that hollow noise
Which (as it through my pipe doth speed)
Bitterns do Carol through a Reed;
In the same key with Monkeys Jiggs,
Or Dirges of Proscribed Piggs,
Or the soft SERENADES above
In calme of Night, when Cats make Love.

    Was ever such a Consort seen!
Fourscore and fourteen with forteen?
Yet sooner they'l agree, One Paire,
Then we in our Spring-Winter Aire;
They may Imbrace, Sigh, Kisse the rest:
Our Breath knows nought but East and West.
Thus have I heard to Childrens Cries
The faire Nurse 'still such Lullabies,
That well all sayd (for what there lay)
The Pleasure did the sorrow pay.

    Sure ther's another way to save
Your Phansie Madam, that's to have
('Tis but a petitioning kinde Fate)
The Organs sent to Bilingsgate;
Where they to that soft murm'ring Quire
Shall teach you All you can admire!

  Or do but heare, how Love-bang KATE
In Pantry darke for freage of Mate,
With edge of steele the square wood shapes,
And DIDO to it chaunts or scrapes.
The merry PHAETON oth' Carre
You'l vow makes a melodious Jarre;
Sweeter and sweeter whisleth He
To un-anointed Axel-tree;
Such swift notes he and 's wheels do run;
For me, I yeeld him PHŒBUS son.

  Say, faire COMANDRES, can it be
You should Ordaine a Mutinie?
For where I howle, all Accents fall,
As Kings Harangues, to *One and All.*
ULYSSES art is now withstood:
You ravish both with Sweet and Good;
Saint SYREN sing, for I dare heare,
But when I Ope', Oh stop your Eare.

  Far lesse be't ÆMULATION
To passe me, or in trill or Tone,
Like the thin throat of PHILOMEL,
And the smart Lute who should excell,
As if her soft Chords should begin,
And strive for sweetnes with the Pin.

  Yet can I Musick too; but such
As is beyond all Voice or Touch;
My minde can in faire Order Chime,
Whilst my true Heart still beats the Time;
My Soule so full of Harmonie,
That it with all parts can agree:
If you winde up to the highest Fret,
It shall descend an Eight from it,
And when you shall vouchsafe to fall
Sixteene above you it shall call,

And yet, so dis-assenting One,
They both shall meet in Unison.

    Come then, bright Cherubin begin!
My loudest Musick is within.
Take all notes with your skillfull Eyes,
Hearke, if mine do not sympathise!
Sound all my thoughts, and see exprest
The *Tablature* of my large Brest;
Then you'l admit, that I too can
Musick above dead sounds of Man;
Such as alone doth blesse the Spheres,
Not to be Reacht with humane Eares.

Valiant Love

Now fie upon that everlasting Life! I Dye!
    She hates! Ah me! It makes me mad;
As if love fir'd his Torch at a moist Eye,
    Or with his Joyes e're Crown'd the sad.
Oh, let me live and shout, when I fall on;
    Let me ev'n Triumph in the first attempt!
Loves Duellist from Conquest's not exempt,
    When his fair Murdresse shall not gain one groan,
And He expire ev'n in Ovation.

II.
Let me make my approach, when I lye downe
    With counter-wrought and Travers Eyes;
With Peals of Confidence Batter the Towne:
    Had ever Beggar yet the Keyes?
No, I will vary stormes with Sun and Winde;
    Be rough, and offer Calme Condition,
March in (and pray't) or starve the Garrison.
    Let her make sallies hourely, yet I'le find
(Though all beat of) shee's to be undermin'd.

III.

Then may it please your *Little Excellence*
    Of Hearts, t' ordaine, by sound of Lips,
That henceforth none in Tears dare Love comence
    (Her thoughts ith' full, his, in th' Eclipse);
On paine of having's Launce broke on her Bed,
    That he be branded all Free Beauties slave,
And his own hollow eyes be domb'd his grave:
    Since in your Hoast that Coward nere was fed,
Who to his Prostrate ere was Prostrated.

The Apostacy of one, and but one Lady

That Frantick Errour I Adore,
    And am confirm'd the Earth turns Round;
Now satisfied O're and o're,
    As rowling Waves, so flowes the Ground,
And as her Neighbour reels the shore:
    Finde such a Woman says she loves,
She's that fixt Heav'n which never moves.

II.

In Marble, Steele, or Porphyrie,
    Who carves or stampes his Armes or Face,
Lookes it by Rust or Storme must dye:
    This Womans Love no Time can raze,
Hardned like Ice in the Sun's Eye,
    Or Your Reflection in a Glasse,
Which keepes possession, though you passe.

III.

We not behold a Watches hand
    To stir, nor Plants or Flowers to grow:
Must we infer that this doth stand,
    And therefore, that those do not blow?

This she acts Calmer, like Heav'ns Brand,
    The stedfast Lightning, slow Loves Dart,
She kils, but ere we feele the smart.

IV.

Oh, she is Constant as the Winde,
    That Revels in an Ev'nings Aire!
Certaine, as Wayes unto the Blinde,
    More reall then her Flatt'ries are;
Gentle, as Chaines that Honour binde,
    More faithfull then an Hebrew Jew,
But as the Divel not halfe so true.

To My Lady H.
Ode

I.

Tell me, ye subtill Judges in Loves Treasury,
    Inform me, which hath most inricht mine eye,
This Diamonds greatnes, or its Clarity?

II.

Ye cloudy spark lights, whose vast multitude
Of Fires, are harder to be found then view'd;
Waite on this Star in her *first Magnitude*.

III.

Calmely or roughly! Ah, she shines too much!
That now I lye, (her influence is such)
Crusht with too strong a hand, or soft a touch.

IV.

Lovers, beware! a certaine, double harme
Waits your proud hopes, her looks al killing charm
Guarded by her as true Victorious Arme.

V.

Thus with her Eyes brave TAMYRIS spake dread,
Which when the Kings dull Breast not entered,
Finding she could not looke, she strook him dead.

La Bella Bona Roba

I.

I cannot tell, who loves the Skeleton
Of a poor Marmoset, nought but boan, boan.
Give me a nakednesse, with her cloath's on.

II.

Such, whose white-sattin upper coat of skin,
Cut upon Velvet rich Incarnadin,
Has yet a Body (and of Flesh) within.

III.

Sure, it is meant good Husbandry in men,
Who do incorporate with Aëry leane,
T' repair their sides, and get their Ribb agen.

IV.

Hard hap unto that Huntsman, that Decrees
Fat joys for all his swet, when as he sees,
After his 'Say, nought but his Keepers Fees.

V.

Then Love I beg, when next thou tak'st thy Bow,
Thy angry shafts, and dost Heart-chasing go,
Passe *Rascall Deare*, strike me the largest Doe.

A La Bourbon
Done moy plus de pitié ou plus de Creaulté,
car sans ce le ne puis pas vivre, ne morir.

I.

Divine Destroyer pitty me no more,
    Or else more pitty me;
Give me more Love, Ah quickly give me more,
    Or else more Cruelty!
      For left thus as I am,
      My Heart is Ice and Flame;
    And languishing thus I
    Can neither Live nor Dye!

II.

Your Glories are Eclipst, and hidden in the Grave
    Of this indifferency;
And, CÆLIA, you can neither Altars have,
    Nor I, a Diety:
      They are Aspects Divine,
      That still, or smile, or shine,
    Or like th' Offended Sky,
    Frowne Death Immediately.

The faire Begger

1.

Commanding Asker, if it be
    Pity that you fain would have,
Then I turn Begger unto thee,
   And aske the thing that thou dost crave;
I will suffice thy hungry need
So thou wilt but my Fancy feed.

II.

In all ill yeares, wa'st ever knowne
   On so much beauty such a dearth?
Which in that thrice-bequeathed gowne
   Looks like the Sun Eclipst with Earth,
Like Gold in Canvas, or with dirt
Unsoyled Ermins close begirt?

III.

Yet happy he that can but tast
   This whiter skin who thirsty is,
Fools dote on sattin motions lac'd,
   The Gods go naked in their blisse,
At th' Barrell's head there shines the Vine,
There only relishes the Wine.

IV.

There quench my heat, and thou shalt sup,
   Worthy the lips that it must touch:
NECTAR from out the starry Cup,
   I beg thy breath not halfe so much;
So both our wants supplied shall be,
You'l give for Love, I Charity.

V.

Cheape then, are pearle-imbroideries
   That not adorne, but cloud thy wast;
Thou shalt be cloath'd above all prise,
   If thou wilt promise me imbrac't;
Wee'l ransack neither Chest or Shelfe,
I'll cover thee with mine own selfe.

VI.

But, Cruel, if thou dost deny
   This necessary almes to me;
What soft-soul'd man but with his Eye
   And hand will hence be shut to thee?

Since all must judge you more unkinde;
I starve your Body, you my minde.

To Ellinda
upon his late recovery
A Paradox

I.
How I grieve that I am well!
    All my Health was in my sicknes,
Go then Destiny, and tell
    Very Death is in this quicknes.

II.
Such a Fate rules over me
    That I glory when I languish,
And do blesse the remedy
    That doth feed, not quench my anguish.

III.
'Twas a gentle warmth that ceas'd
    In the Vizard of a feavor;
But I feare now I am eas'd
    All the flames since I must leave her.

IV.
Joyes though witherd, circled me,
    When unto her voice inured,
Like those who by Harmony
    Only can be throughly Cured.

V.
Sweet, sure, was that Malady,
    Whilst the pleasant Angel hover'd,
Which ceasing they are all as I,
    Angry that they are recover'd.

VI.

And as men in Hospitals,
   That are maim'd, are lodg'd and dined;
But when once their danger fals,
   Ah, th' are healed to be pined!

VII.

Fainting so I might before
   Sometime have the leave to hand her,
But lusty, am beat out of dore,
   And for Love compell'd to wander.

AMYNTOR *from beyond the Sea to* ALEXIS
A Dialogue

AMYNTOR.
ALEXIS! ah ALEXIS! can it be,
   Though so much wet and drie
      Doth drowne our Eye,
Thou keep'st thy winged voice from me?

ALEXIS.
AMYNTOR, a profounder sea, I feare,
   Hath swallow'd me, where now
      My armes do row,
I floate i' th' Ocean of a Teare.

LUCASTA weepes, lest I look back and tread
   Your watry Land againe.
  AMYNT. I'd through the raine;
   Such showrs are quickly over-spread.

IV

Conceive how Joy, after this short divorce,
   Will circle her with beames,

When, like your streames,
You shall rowle back with kinder force?

V

And call the helping winds to vent your thought.
    Alex. Amyntor! Chloris! where,
        Or in what Sphere
   Say, may that glorious faire be sought?

Amyntor.

She's now the center of these armes e're blest
    Whence may she never move,
       Till Time and Love
   Haste to their everlasting rest.

Alexis.

Ah subtile swaine! doth not my flame rise high
    As yours, and burne as hot?
       Am not I shot
   With the selfe same Artillery?

VIII

And can I breath without her air? **Amyn.** Why, then,
    From thy tempestuous Earth,
      Where blood and dearth
   Raigne 'stead of Kings, agen

Wafte thy selfe over, and lest storms from far
    Arise, bring in our sight
      The Seas delight,
 Lucasta that bright Northerne star.

Alexis.

But as we cut the rugged deepe, I feare
    The green-God stops his fell
      Chariot of shell,
  And smooths the maine to ravish her.

Amyntor.
Oh no, the Prince of waters fires are done,
  He as his Empire Old,
    And Rivers Cold;
 His Queen now runs abed to th' Sun;

XII
But all his treasure he shall ope' that day:
  Tritons shall sound, his fleete
    In silver meete,
 And to her their rich offrings pay.

Alexis.
We flye, Amyntor, not amaz'd how sent
  By Water, Earth, or Aire:
    Or if with her
    By Fire, ev'n there
 I move in mine owne Element.

A Lady with a Falcon on her fist
To the Honourable my Cousin A. L.

I.
This Queen of Prey (now Prey to you),
  Fast to that Pirch of Ivory
In silver Chaines and silken Clue
  Hath now made full thy Victory:

II.
The swelling Admirall of the dread
  Cold Deepe, burnt in thy Flames, Oh Faire!
Wast not enough, but thou must lead
  Bound too the Princesse of the Aire?

III.

Unarm'd of Wings and Scaly Oare,
    Unhappy Crawler on the Land,
To what Heav'n fly'st? div'st to what Shoare,
    That her brave Eyes do not command?

IV.

Ascend the Chariot of the Sun
    From her bright pow'r to shelter thee:
Her Captive (Foole) outgases him;
    Ah, what lost wretches then are we!

V.

Now, proud Usurpers on the Right
    Of sacred Beauty, heare your dombe;
Recant your SEX, your MASTRY, MIGHT;
    Lower you cannot be or'ecome:

VI.

Repent, ye er'e nam'd HE or HEAD,
    For y' are in Falcons Monarchy,
And in that just Dominion bred,
    In which the NOBLER is the SHEE.

Calling LUCASTA *from Her Retirement*
Ode

I.

From the dire Monument of thy black roome
    Wher now that vestal flame thou dost intombe
As in the inmost Cell of all Earths Wombe,

II.

Sacred LUCASTA like the pow'rfull ray
Of Heavenly Truth, passe this Cimmerian way,
Whilst all the Standards of your beames display.

III.

Arise and climbe our whitest, highest Hill,
There your sad thoughts with joy and wonder fill,
And see Seas calme as Earth, Earth as your Will.

IV.

Behold! how lightning like a Taper flyes
And guilds your Chari't, but ashamed dyes
Seeing it selfe out-gloried by your Eyes.

V.

Threatning and boystrous tempests gently bow,
And to your steps part in soft paths, when now
There no where hangs a Cloud, but on your brow.

VI.

No showrs but 'twixt your lids, nor gelid snow,
But what your whiter, chaster brest doth ow,
Whilst winds in Chains colder for sorrow blow.

VII.

Shrill Trumpets now doe only sound to Eate,
Artillery hath loaden ev'ry dish with meate,
And Drums at ev'ry Health Alarmes beate.

VIII.

All things LUCASTA, but LUCASTA call,
Trees borrow Tongues, Waters in accents fall,
The Aire doth sing, and Fire's Musicall.

IX.

Awake from the dead Vault in which you dwell,
All's Loyall here, except your thoughts rebell,
Which so let loose, often their Gen'rall quell.

X.

See! she obeys! by all obeyed thus;
No storms, heats, Colds, no soules contentious,
Nor Civill War is found —— I meane, to us.

XI.

Lovers and Angels, though in Heav'n they show
And see the Woes and Discords here below,
What they not feele, must not be said to know.

Aramantha

A Pastorall

Up with the jolly Bird of Light
   Who sounds his third Retreat to Night;
Faire *Aramantha* from her bed
Ashamed starts, and rises Red
As the Carnation-mantled Morne,
Who now the blushing Robe doth spurne,
And puts on angry Gray, whilst she,
The *Envy of a Deity*,
Arayes her limbes, too rich indeed
To be inshrin'd in such a Weed;
Yet lovely 'twas and strait, but fit;
Not made for her, but she to it:
By Nature it sate close and free,
As the just bark unto the Tree:
Unlike Loves Martyrs of the Towne,
All day imprison'd in a Gown,
Who, Rackt in Silke 'stead of a Dresse,
Are cloathed in a Frame or Presse,
And with that liberty and room,
The dead expatiate in a Tombe.
   No Cabinets with curious Washes,

Bladders and perfumed Plashes;
No venome-temper'd water's here,
Mercury is banished this Sphere:
Her Payle's all this, in which wet Glasse,
She both doth cleanse and view her Face.

    Far hence, all *Iberian* smells,
Hot Amulets, Pomander spells;
Fragrant Gales, cool Ay'r, the fresh,
And naturall Odour of her Flesh,
Proclaim her sweet from th' Wombe as Morne.
Those colour'd things were made not borne,
Which fixt within their narrow straits,
Do looke like their own counterfeyts.
So like the Provance Rose she walkt,
Flowerd with blush, with verdure stalkt;
Th' Officious Wind her loose Hayre Curles,
The Dewe her happy linnen purles,
But wets a Tresse, which instantly
Sol with a Crisping Beame doth dry.

    Into the Garden is she come,
Love and Delights *Elisium*;
If ever Earth show'd all her Store,
View her discolourd budding Floore;
Here her glad Eye she largely feedes,
And stands 'mongst them, as they 'mong weeds;
The flowers in their best aray,
As to their Queen their Tribute pay,
And freely to her Lap proscribe
A Daughter out of ev'ry Tribe:
Thus as she moves, they all bequeath
At once the Incense of their Breath.

    The noble *Heliotropian*
Now turnes to her, and knowes no Sun;
    And as her glorious face doth vary,
So opens loyall golden *Mary*
Who, if but glanced from her sight,
Straight shuts again, as it were Night.

    The *Violet* (else lost ith' heap)
Doth spread fresh purple for each step;
With whose Humility possest,
Sh' inthrones the *poore Girle* in her breast:
The *July-flow'r* that hereto thriv'd,
Knowing her self no longer-liv'd,
But for one look of her upheaves,
Then 'stead of teares straight sheds her leaves.
    Now the rich robed *Tulip* who,
Clad all in Tissue close doth woe
Her (sweet to th' eye but smelling sower),
She gathers to adorn her Bower.
    But the proud *Hony-suckle* spreads
Like a Pavilion her Heads,
Contemnes the wanting Commonalty,
That but to two ends usefull be,
And to her lips thus aptly plac't,
With *smell* and *Hue* presents her *Tast*.
    So all their due Obedience pay,
Each thronging to be in her Way:
Faire *Aramantha* with her Eye
Thanks those that live, which else would dye:
The rest, in silken fetters bound,
By *Crowning* her are *Crown* and *Crown'd*.
    And now the Sun doth higher rise,
Our *Flora* to the meadow hies:
The poore distressed Heifers low,
And as sh' approacheth gently bow,
Begging her charitable leasure
To strip them of their milkie Treasure.
    Out of the Yeomanry oth' Heard,
With grave aspect, and feet prepar'd,
A rev'rend Lady Cow drawes neare,
Bids *Aramantha* welcome here;
And from her privy purse lets fall
A Pearle or two, which seeme to call
This adorn'd adored Fayry

To the banquet of her Dayry.
    Soft *Aramantha* weeps to see
'Mongst men such inhumanitie,
That those who do receive in Hay,
And pay in silver twice a Day,
Should by their cruell barb'rous theft
Be both of that and life bereft.
    But 'tis decreed, when ere this dies,
That she shall fall a Sacrifice
Unto the Gods, since those that trace
Her stemme, show 'tis a God-like race,
Descending in an even line
From Heifers, and from Steeres divine,
Making the honour'd extract full
In *Io* and *Europa's* Bull.
She was the largest goodliest Beast,
That ever Mead or Altar blest;
Round [w]as her Udder, and more white
Then is the *milkie way* in Night;
Her full broad Eye did sparkle fire,
Her breath was sweet as kind desire,
And in her beauteous crescent shone,
Bright as the Argent-horned Moone.
    But see! this whiteness is obscure,
Cynthia spotted, she impure;
Her body writheld, and her eyes
Departing lights at obsequies:
Her lowing hot to the fresh Gale,
Her breath perfumes the field withall;
To those two Suns that ever shine,
To those plump parts she doth inshrine,
To th' hovering snow of either hand,
That *Love* and *Cruelty* command.
    After the breakfast on her Teat,
She takes her leave oth' mournfull Neat,
Who, by her toucht now prize their life,
Worthy alone the *hallowed knife*.

    Into the neighbring Wood she's gone,
Whose roofe defies the tell-tale Sunne,
And locks out ev'ry prying beame;
Close by the Lips of a cleare streame,
She sits and entertaines her Eye
With the moist Chrystall, and the frye
With burnisht-silver mal'd, whose Oares
Amazed still make to the shoares;
What need she other bait or charm,
But look? or Angle, but her arm?
The happy Captive, gladly ta'n,
Sues ever to be slave in vaine,
Who instantly (confirm'd in's feares)
Hasts to his Element of teares.

    From hence her various windings roave
To a well-orderd stately grove;
This is the Pallace of the Wood,
And Court oth' Royall Oake, where stood
The whole nobility, the Pine,
Strait Ash, tall Firre, and wanton Vine;
The proper Cedar, and the rest;
Here she her deeper senses blest;
Admires great Nature in this Pile
Floor'd with greene-velvet Camomile,
Garnisht with Gems of unset fruit,
Supply'd still with a self recruit;
Her bosom wrought with pretty Eyes
Of never-planted Strawberries;
Where th' winged Musick of the ayre
Do richly feast, and for their fare
Each evening in a silent shade,
Bestow a gratefull *Serenade*.

    Thus ev'n tyerd with delight,
Sated in Soul and Appetite;
Full of the purple plumme and Peare,
The golden Apple with the faire
Grape, that mirth fain would have taught her,

And nuts which Squirrells cracking brought her;
She softly layes her weary limbs,
Whilst gentle slumber now beginnes
To draw the Curtaines of her Eye;
When straight awakend with a Crie
And bitter groan, again reposes,
Again a deep sigh interposes.
And now she heares a trembling Voyce:
Ah can there ought on earth rejoyce!
Why weares she this gay Livery
Not black as her dark entrails be?
Can trees be green, and to the Ay'r
Thus prostitute their flowing Hayr?
Why do they sprout, not witherd dy?
Must each thing live save wretched I?
Can dayes triumph in *blew* and *red*,
When both their *light*, and *life* is fled?
Fly Joy on wings of *Popinjayes*
To Courts of fools, where as your playes
Dye, laught at and forgot; whilst all
That's good, mourns at this Funerall.
Weep, all ye *Graces*, and you sweet
Quire, that at the Hill inspir'd meet:
Love put thy tapers out that we
And th' world may seem as blind as thee:
And be, since she is lost (ah wound!)
Not *Heav'n* it self by any found.

    Now as a Prisoner new cast,
Who sleeps in chaines that night his last,
Next morn is wak't with a repreeve,
And from his trance not dream bid Live;
Wonders (his sence not having scope)
Who speaks, his friend, or his false Hope.

    So *Aramantha* heard, but feare
Dares not yet trust her tempting Eare:
And as againe her arms oth' ground
Spread pillows for her Head, a sound

More dismall makes a swift divorce,
And starts her thus —— Rage, Rapine, Force!
Ye blew-flam'd daughters oth' Abysse,
Bring all your Snakes, here let them hisse;
Let not a leaf its freshnesse keep;
Blast all their roots, and as you creepe
And leave behind your deadly slime,
Poyson the budding branch in's prime:
Wast the proud Bowers of this Grove,
That Fiends may dwell in it, and move
As in their proper Hell, whilst she
Above laments this Tragedy:
Yet pities not our Fate; Oh faire
Vow-breaker, now betroth'd to th' Ay'r;
Why by those Lawes did we not die,
As live but one, *Lucasta* ! why——
As he *Lucasta* nam'd, a groan
Strangles the fainting passing tone;
But as she heard, *Lucasta* smiles,
Posses her round, she's slipt mean whiles
Behind the blind of a thick Bush,
When, each word temp'ring with a blush,
She gently thus bespake: Sad swaine,
If mates in woe do ease our pain,
Here's one full of that antick grief,
Which stifled would for ever live,
But told, expires; pray then, reveale
(To show our wound is half to heale),
What Mortall Nymph or Deity
Bewail you thus? Who ere you be,
The Shepheard sight, my woes I crave
Smotherd in me, I in my Grave;
Yet be in show or truth a Saint,
Or fiend, breath *Anthemes*, heare my plaint
For her and thy breath's symphony,
Which now makes full the Harmony
Above, and to whose voice the Spheres

Listen, and call her Musick theirs;
This was I blest on earth with, so
As *Druids* amorous did grow,
Jealous of both: for as one day
This *Star*, as yet but set in *clay*,
By an imbracing River lay,
They steept her in the hollowed brooke
Which from her humane nature tooke,
And straight to heaven with winged feare,
Thus *ravisht* with her, *ravish* her.

    The Nymph reply'd, this holy rape
Became the Gods, whose obscure shape
They cloth'd with light, whilst ill you grieve
Your better life should ever live,
And weep that she, to whom you wish
What Heav'n could give, has all its blisse;
Calling her Angell here, yet be
Sad at this true divinity:
She's for the *Altar*, not the *skies*,
Whom first you *crowne*, then *sacrifice*.

    Fond man thus to a precipice
Aspires, till at the top his eyes
Have lost the safety of the plain,
Then begs of Fate the vales againe.

    The now confounded Shepheard cries:
Ye all-confounding Destines!
How did you make that voice so sweet
Without that glorious form to it?
Thou sacred spirit of my Deare
Where e're thou hoverst o're us hear!
Imbark thee in the Lawrell tree,
And a new Phebus follows thee,
Who, 'stead of all his burning rayes
Will strive to catch thee with his layes;
Or, if within the Orient Vine,
Thou art both Deity and Wine;
But if thou takest the mirtle grove,

That *Paphos* is, thou *Queene of Love*
And I, thy swain who (else) must die,
By no Beasts, but thy cruelty:
But you are rougher than the Winde,
Are Souls on *Earth* then *Heav'n* more kind?
Imprisoned in Mortality
Lucasta would have answered me.
Lucasta! Aramantha said,
Is she that Virgin-star a Maid,
Except her prouder Livery,
In beauty poore, and cheap as I?
Whose glory like a Meteor shone,
Or aëry Apparition
Admir'd a while but slighted known.

    Fierce, as the chased lyon hies,
He rowses him, and to her flies,
Thinking to answer with his Speare ——
    Now, as in warre intestine, where
Ith' mist of a black Battell, each
Layes at his next, then makes a breach
Through th' entrayles of another whom
He sees nor knows whence he did come
Guided alone by Rage and th' Drumme,
But stripping and impatient wild,
He finds too soon his onely child.
    So our expiring desp'rate Lover
Far'd, when amaz'd he did discover
Lucasta in this Nymph, his sinne
Darts the accursed Javelin
'Gainst his own breast, which she puts by
With a soft Lip and gentle Eye,
Then closes with him on the ground
And now her smiles have heal'd his wound.
Alexis too again is found:
But not untill those heavy Crimes
She hath kis'd off a thousand times,
Who not contented with this pain

Doth threaten to offend again.
    And now they gaze, and sigh, and weep,
Whilst each cheek doth the other's steep,
Whilst tongues as exorcis'd are calm;
Onely the Rhet'rick of the Palm
Prevailing pleads, untill at last
They chain'd in one another fast:
Lucasta to him doth relate
Her various chance and diffring fate:
How chac'd by Hydraphil, and tract
The num'rous foe to Philanact,
Who whilst they for the same things fight,
As Bards Decrees, and Druids rite,
For safeguard of their proper joyes,
And Shepheards freedome, each destroyes
The glory of this Sicilie;
Since seeking thus the remedie,
They fancy (building on false ground)
The means must them and it confound,
Yet are resolv'd to stand or fall,
And win a little or lose all.
    From this sad storm of fire and blood
She fled to this yet living Wood;
Where she 'mongst savage beasts doth find
Her self more safe then humane kind.
    Then She relates, how Cælia—
The Lady here strippes her array,
And girdles her in home spunne bayes,
Then makes her conversant in Layes
Of birds, and swaines more innocent
That kenne not guile or courtshipment.
    Now walks she to her bow'r to dine
Under a shade of Eglantine,
Upon a dish of Natures cheere
Which both grew drest, and serv'd up there:
That done, she feasts her smell with Po'ses
Pluckt from the Damask cloth of Roses.

Which there continually doth stay,
And onely frost can take away;
Then wagers which hath most content
Her eye, eare, hand, her gust or sent.

    Intranc't ALEXIS sees and heares,
As walking above all the spheres:
Knows and adores this, and is wilde
Untill with her he live thus milde.
So that, which to his thoughts he meant
For losse of her a punishment,
His armes hung up and his Sword broke,
His Ensignes folded, he betook
Himself unto the humble Crook:
And for a full reward of all,
She now doth him her shepheard call,
And in a SEE of flow'rs install:
Then gives her faith immediately,
Which he returns religiously;
Both vowing in her peacefull Cave
To make their Bridall-bed and grave.

    But the true joy this pair conceiv'd,
Each from the other first bereav'd,
And then found, after such alarmes,
Fast-pinion'd in each others armes,
Ye panting Virgins, that do meet
Your Loves within their winding-sheet,
Breathing and constant still ev'n there;
Or souls their bodies in yon' sphere,
Or Angels men return'd from Hell,
And separated mindes can tell.

Lucasta: Posthume Poems

Her Reserved looks

*L*ucasta, frown, and let me die,
   But smile, and see, I live;
The sad indifference of your Eye
   Both kills and doth reprieve.
You hide our fate within its screen,
   We feel our judgment, ere we hear:
So in one Picture I have seen
   An Angel here, the Divel there.

Lucasta laughing

Hark, how she laughs aloud,
   Although the world put on its shrowd:
  Wept at by the fantastic Crowd,
    Who cry: One drop, let fall
From her, might save the Universal Ball.
     She laughs again
    At our ridiculous pain;
And at our merry misery
     She laughs, until she cry;
     Sages, forbear
    That ill-contrived tear,
     Although your fear,
Doth barricadoe Hope from your soft Ear.
That which still makes her mirth to flow,
   Is our sinister-handed woe,
Which downwards on its head doth go;
   And, ere that it is sown, doth grow.
      This makes her spleen contract,
     And her just pleasure feast;
      For the unjustest act
     Is still the pleasant'st jest.

SONG

1

Strive not, vain Lover, to be fine;
Thy silk's the Silk-worms, and not thine;
You lessen to a Fly your Mistris Thought,
To think it may be in a Cobweb caught.
What though her thin transparent lawn
Thy heart in a strong Net hath drawn?
Not all the arms the God of Fire ere made,
Can the soft Bulwarks of nak'd LOVE invade.

2

Be truly fine then, and your self dress
In her fair Souls immac'late glass:
Then by reflection you may have the bliss
Perhaps to see what a True fineness is;
When all your Gawderies will fit
Those only that are poor in wit:
She that a *clinquant* outside doth adore,
Dotes on a gilded *Statue*, and no more.

In Allusion to the *French Song* '*N'entendez vous pas ce language*'

Cho.
Then understand you not (Fair choice)
this Language without tongue or voice?

I.

How often have my Tears
Invaded your soft Ears,
And dropp'd their silent Chimes
A thousand thousand times,
Whilst Echo did your eyes,

  And sweetly Sympathize;
  But that the wary Lid
  Their Sluces did forbid?
Cho. *Then understand you not (Fair choice)*
  This Language without tongue or voice?

II.

  My Arms did plead my wound,
  Each in the other bound;
  Volleys of Sighs did crowd,
  And ring my griefs alowd;
  Grones, like a Canon Ball,
  Batter'd the Marble Wall,
  That the kind Neighb'ring Grove,
  Did mutiny for Love.
Cho. *Then understand you not (Fair choice)*
  This Language without tongue or voice?

III.

  The Rheth'rick of my Hand
  Woo'd you to understand;
  Nay, in our silent walk
  My very Feet would talk,
  My Knees were eloquent,
  And spake the Love I meant;
  But deaf unto that Ayr,
  They bent, would fall in Prayer.
Cho. *Then understand you not (Fair choice)*
  This Language without tongue or voice?

IV.

  No? Know then I would melt,
  On every Limb I felt,
  And on each naked part
  Spread my expanded Heart,
  That not a Vein of thee,
  But should be fill'd with mee.

Whilst on thine own Down, I
　　　Would tumble, pant, and dye.
Cho. *Then understand you not (Fair choice)*
　　　This Language without tongue or voice?

Night. *To* Lucasta

Night! loathed Jaylor of the lock'd up Sun,
　　And Tyrant-turnkey on committed day;
Bright Eyes lye fettered in thy Dungeon,
　　And Heaven it self doth thy dark Wards obey:
　　　　Thou dost arise our living Hell,
　　　　With thee grones, terrors, furies dwell,
　　　　Until *Lucasta* doth awake,
And with her Beams these heavy chaines off shake.

Behold, with opening her Almighty Lid
　　Bright eyes break rowling, and with lustre spread,
　　And captive Day his chariot mounted is;
　　　　Night to her proper Hell is beat,
　　　　And scrued to her Ebon Seat;
　　　　Till th' Earth with play oppressed lies,
And drawes again the Curtains of her Eyes.

But Bondslave, I, know neither Day nor Night;
　　Whether she murth'ring sleep or saving wake;
　　Now broyl'd ith' Zone of her reflected light,
　　　　Then frose my Isicles, not Sinews shake:
　　　　Smile then new Nature, your soft blast
　　　　Doth melt our Ice, and Fires wast:
Whil'st the scorch'd shiv'ring world new born
Now feels it all the day one rising morn.

Love Inthron'd

Ode

I n troth, I do my self perswade,
   That the wilde boy is grown a Man;
And all his Childishnesse off laid,
    E're since *Lucasta* did his fires Fan;
      H' has left his apish Jigs,
        And whipping Hearts like Gigs;
    For t'other day I heard him swear
That Beauty should be crown'd in Honours Chair.

II.

With what a true and heavenly State
    He doth his glorious Darts dispence,
Now cleans'd from Falshood, Blood, and Hate,
    And newly tipt with Innocence;
      Love Justice is become,
        And doth the Cruel doome:
    Reversed is the old Decree;
Behold! he sits Inthron'd with Majestie.

III.

Inthroned in *Lucasta's* Eye,
    He doth our Faith and Hearts Survey;
Then measures them by Sympathy,
    And each to th' others Breast convey;
      Whilst to his Altars Now
        The frozen Vestals Bow,
    And strickt *Diana* too doth go
A hunting with his fear'd, exchanged Bow.

IV.

Th' Imbracing Seas and Ambient Air,
    Now in his holy fires burn;
Fish couple, Birds and Beasts in pair,

Do their own Sacrifices turn:
   This is a Miracle,
   That might Religion swell:
But she that these and their God awes,
Her crowned Self submits to her own Laws.

Her Muffe

'Twas not for some calm blessing to receive,
   Thou didst thy polish'd hands in shagg'd furs weave;
     It were no blessing thus obtain'd,
     Thou rather would'st a curse have gain'd,
Then let thy warm driven snow be ever stain'd.

II.

Not that you feared the discolo'ring cold
Might alchymize their Silver into Gold;
     Nor could your ten white Nuns so sin,
     That you should thus pennance them in
Each in her coarse hair smock of Discipline.

III.

Nor, *Hero*-like who, on their crest still wore
A Lyon, Panther, Leopard or a Bore,
     To looke their Enemies in their Herse;
     Thou would'st thy hand should deeper pierce,
And, in its softness rough, appear more fierce.

IV.

No, no, *Lucasta*, destiny Decreed
That beasts to thee a sacrifice should bleed,
     And strip themselves to make you gay;
     For ne'r yet herald did display,
A Coat, where *Sables* upon *Ermin* lay.

V.

This for Lay-Lovers, that must stand at dore,
Salute the threshold, and admire no more:
    But I, in my Invention tough,
    Rate not this outward bliss enough,
But still contemplate must the hidden Muffe.

A Black patch on Lucasta*'s Face*

Dull as I was, to think that a Court Fly,
    Presumed so near her Eye,
    When 'twas th' industrious Bee
Mistook her glorious Face for Paradise,
To sum up all his Chymistry of Spice;
    With a brave pride and honour led,
    Near both her Suns he makes his bed;
And though a Spark struggles to rise as red:
        Then Æmulates the gay
        Daughter of Day,
    Acts the *Romantick Phœnix* fate;
When now, with all his Sweets lay'd out in state,
    Lucasta scatters but one Heat,
And all the Aromatick pills do sweat,
And Gums calcin'd, themselves to powder beat;
    Which a fresh gale of Air
    Conveys into her Hair;
    Then chast he's set on fire,
And in these holy flames doth glad expire;
    And that black marble Tablet there
    So near her either Sphere,
    Was placed; nor foyl, nor Ornament,
But the sweet little Bees large Monument.

Another

As I beheld a Winters Evening Air,
Curl'd in her court false locks of living hair,
Butter'd with Jessamine the Sun left there,

II.
Galliard and clinquant she appear'd to give,
A Serenade or Ball to us that grieve,
And teach us *A la mode* more gently live.

III.
But as a *Moor*, who to her Cheeks prefers
White spots t'allure her black Idolaters,
Me thought she look'd all ore bepatch'd with Stars;

IV.
Like the dark front of some *Ethiopian* Queen,
Vailed all ore with Gems of Red, Blew, Green;
Whose ugly Night seem'd masked with days Skreen;

V.
Whilst the fond people offer'd Sacrifice
To Saphyrs 'stead of Veins and Arteries,
And bow'd unto the Diamonds, not her Eyes.

VI.
Behold *Lucasta*'s face, how't glows like Noon!
A Sun intire is her complexion,
And form'd of one whole Constellation.

VII.
So gently shining, so serene, so cleer,
Her look doth Universal Nature cheer;
Only a cloud or two hangs here and there.

To Lucasta I

I Laugh and sing, but cannot tell
Whether the folly on't sounds well;
          But then I groan,
          Methinks in Tune,
Whilst Grief, Despair, and Fear, dance to the Air
      Of my despised Prayer.

        II.
A pretty Antick Love does this,
Then strikes a Galliard with a Kiss;
          As in the end
          The Chords they rend;
So you but with a touch from your fair Hand,
      Turn all to Saraband.

To Lucasta II

Like to the Sent'nel Stars, I watch all Night;
    For still the grand round of your Light,
        And glorious Breast
        Awake in me an East,
Nor will my rolling Eyes ere know a West.

      II.
Now on my Down I'm toss'd as on a Wave,
    And my repose is made my Grave;
        Fluttering I lye,
        Do beat my Self and dye,
But for a Resurrection from your eye.

      III.
Ah, my fair Murdresse! dost thou cruelly heal,
    With Various pains to make me well?

Then let me be
Thy cut Anatomie,
And in each mangled part my heart you'l see.

Lucasta *at the Bath*

I 'th' Autumn of a Summers day,
When all the Winds got leave to play;
Lucasta, that fair Ship, is lanch'd,
And from its crust this Almond blanch'd.

II.
Blow then, unruly Northwind, blow,
'Till in their holds your Eyes you stow;
And swell your Cheeks, bequeath chill Death:
See! she hath smil'd thee out of Breath.

III.
Court gentle *Zephyr*, court and fan
Her softer breast's carnation Wan;
Your charming Rhethorick of Down
Flyes scatter'd from before her frown.

IV.
Say, my white Water-Lilly, say,
How is't those warm streams break away?
Cut by thy chast cold breast which dwells
Amidst them arm'd in Isicles.

V.
And the hot floods, more raging grown
In flames of Thee, then in their own,
In their distempers wildly glow,
And kisse thy Pillar of fix'd Snow.

VI.

No Sulphur, through whose each blew Vein
The thick and lazy Currents strein,
Can cure the Smarting, nor the fell
Blisters of Love wherewith they swell.

VII.

These great Physicians of the Blind,
The Lame, and fatal Blains of *Inde*,
In every drop themselves now see
Speckled with a new Leprosie.

VIII.

As Sick drinks are with old Wine dash'd,
Foul Waters too with Spirits wash'd;
Thou greiv'd, perchance, one tear let'st fall,
Which straight did purifie them all.

IX.

And now is cleans'd enough the flood,
Which since runs cleare, as doth thy blood;
Of the wet Pearls uncrown thy hair,
And mantle thee with *Ermin* air.

X.

Lucasta, hail! fair Conqueresse
Of Fire, Air, Earth and Seas;
Thou whom all kneel to, yet even thou
Wilt unto Love, thy captive, bow.

The Ant

Forbear, thou great good Husband, little Ant;
 A little respite from thy flood of sweat;
Thou, thine own Horse and Cart, under this Plant

Thy spacious tent, fan thy prodigious heat;
Down with thy double load of that one grain;
It is a Granarie for all thy Train.

II.

Cease large example of wise thrift a while
    (For thy example is become our Law)
And teach thy frowns a seasonable smile:
    So *Cato* sometimes the nak'd Florals saw.
And thou almighty foe, lay by thy sting,
Whilst thy unpay'd Musicians, Crickets, sing.

III.

Lucasta, She that holy makes the Day,
    And 'stills new Life in fields of Fueillemort:
Hath back restor'd their Verdure with one Ray,
    And with her Eye bid all to play and sport.
Ant, to work still; Age will Thee Truant call;
And to save now, th' art worse than prodigal.

IV.

Austere and *Cynick* ! not one hour t'allow,
    To lose with pleasure what thou gotst with pain:
But drive on sacred Festivals, thy Plow;
    Tearing high-ways with thy ore-charged Wain.
Not all thy life time one poor Minute live,
And thy o're labour'd Bulk with mirth relieve?

V.

Look up then miserable Ant, and spie
    Thy fatal foes, for breaking of her Law,
Hov'ring above thee, Madam, *Margaret Pie*:
    And her fierce Servant, Meagre, Sir *John Daw*:
Thy Self and Storehouse now they do store up,
And thy whole harvest too within their Crop.

VI.
Thus we unthrifty thrive within Earths Tomb
    For some more rav'nous and ambitious Jaw:
The *Grain* in th' *Ants*, the *Ants* in the *Pies* womb,
    The *Pie* in th' *Hawks*, the *Hawks* ith' *Eagles* maw:
So scattering to hord 'gainst a long Day,
Thinking to save all, we cast all away.

The Snayl

Wise Emblem of our Politick World,
    Sage Snayl, within thine own self curl'd;
Instruct me softly to make hast,
Whilst these my Feet go slowly fast.
    Compendious Snayl! thou seem'st to me,
Large *Euclids* strict Epitome;
And in each Diagram dost Fling
Thee from the point unto the Ring.
A Figure now Triangulare,
An Oval now, and now a Square;
And then a Serpentine dost crawl
Now a straight Line, now crook'd, now all.
    Preventing Rival of the Day,
Th'art up and openest thy Ray,
And ere the Morn cradles the Moon,
Th'art broke into a Beauteous Noon.
Then when the Sun sups in the Deep,
Thy Silver Horns ere *Cinthia's* peep;
And thou from thine own liquid Bed
New *Phœbus* heav'st thy pleasant Head.
    Who shall a Name for thee create,
Deep Riddle of Mysterious State?
Bold Nature that gives common Birth
To all products of Seas and Earth,
Of thee, as Earth-quakes, is affraid,
Nor will thy dire Deliv'ry aid.

  Thou thine own daughter then, and Sire,
That Son and Mother art intire,
That big still with thy self dost go,
And liv'st an aged Embrio;
That like the Cubbs of *India*,
Thou from thyself a while dost play:
But frighted with a Dog or Gun,
In thine own Belly thou dost run,
And as thy House was thine own womb,
So thine own womb, concludes thy tomb.
  But now I must (analys'd King)
Thy Œconomic Virtues sing;
Thou great stay'd Husband still within,
Thou, thee, that's thine dost Discipline;
And when thou art to progress bent,
Thou mov'st thy self and tenement,
As Warlike *Scythians* travayl'd, you
Remove your Men and City too;
Then after a sad Dearth and Rain,
Thou scatterest thy Silver Train;
And when the Trees grow nak'd and old,
Thou cloathest them with Cloth of Gold,
Which from thy Bowels thou dost spin,
And draw from the rich Mines within.
  Now hast thou chang'd thee Saint; and made
Thy self a Fane that's cupula'd;
And in thy wreathed Cloister thou
Walkest thine own Gray fryer too;
Strict, and lock'd up, th'art Hood all ore
And ne'er Eliminat'st thy Dore.
On Sallads thou dost feed severe,
And 'stead of beads thou dropp'st a tear,
And when to rest, each calls the Bell,
Thou sleep'st within thy Marble Cell;
Where in dark contemplation plac'd,
The sweets of Nature thou dost tast;
Who now with Time thy days resolve,

And in a Jelly thee dissolve.
Like a shot Star, which doth repair
Upward, and Rarifie the Air.

Another

The Centaur, Syren, I foregoe,
  Those have been sung, and lowdly too;
Nor of the mixed Sphynx Ile write,
Nor the renown'd Hermaphrodite:
Behold! this Huddle doth appear
Of Horses, Coach, and Charioteer;
That moveth him by traverse Law,
And doth himself both drive and draw;
Then when the Sun the South doth winne,
He baits him hot in his own Inne;
I heard a grave and austere Clark,
Resolv'd him Pilot both and Barque;
That like the fam'd ship of *Trevere*,
Did on the Shore himself Lavere:
Yet the Authentick do beleeve,
Who keep their Judgement in their Sleeve,
That he is his own Double man,
And sick, still carries his Sedan:
Or that like Dames i' th Land of Luyck,
He wears his everlasting Huyck:
But banisht, I admire his fate
Since neither Ostracisme of State,
Nor a perpetual exile,
Can force this Virtue change his Soyl;
For wheresoever he doth go,
He wanders with his Country too.

Courante Monsieur

That frown, *Aminta*, now hath drown'd
    Thy bright front's power, and crown'd
        Me that was bound.
  No, no, deceived Cruel no!
        Loves fiery darts,
Till tipt with kisses, never kindle Hearts.

  Adieu, weak beauteous Tyrant, see!
    Thy angry flames meant me,
        Retort on thee:
  For know, it is decreed, proud fair,
        I ne'r must dye
By any scorching, but a melting Eye.

A loose Saraband

Nay, prethee, Dear, draw nigher,
  Yet closer, nigher yet;
Here is a double Fire,
  A dry one and a wet:
True lasting Heavenly Fuel
Puts out the Vestal jewel,
When once we twining marry
Mad Love with wilde Canary.

        II.
Off with that crowned Venice,
  'Till all the House doth flame,
Wee'l quench it straight in Rhenish,
  Or what we must not name:
Milk lightning still asswageth,
So when our fury rageth,
As th' only means to cross it,
Wee'l drown it in Love's posset.

III.

Love never was Well-willer,
    Unto my Nag or mee,
Ne'r watter'd us ith' Cellar,
    But the cheap Buttery:
At th' head of his own Barrells,
Where broach'd are all his Quarrels,
Should a true noble Master
Still make his Guest his Taster.

IV.

See, all the World how't staggers,
    More ugly drunk then we,
As if far gone in daggers,
    And blood it seem'd to be:
We drink our glass of Roses,
Which nought but sweets discloses:
Then in our Loyal Chamber,
Refresh us with Loves Amber.

V.

Now tell me, thou fair Cripple,
    That dumb canst scarcely see
Th' almightinesse of Tipple,
    And th' ods 'twixt thee and thee:
What of Elizium's missing?
Still Drinking and still Kissing;
Adoring plump *October*;
Lord! what is Man and Sober?

VI.

Now, is there such a Trifle
    As Honour, the fools Gyant?
What is there left to rifle,
    When Wine makes all parts plyant?
Let others Glory follow,
In their false riches wallow,

And with their grief be merry;
Leave me but Love and Sherry.

The Falcon

Fair Princesse of the spacious Air,
That hast vouchsaf'd acquaintance here,
With us are quarter'd below stairs,
That can reach Heav'n with nought but Pray'rs;
Who, when our activ'st wings we try,
Advance a foot into the Sky.

    Bright heir t' th' Bird Imperial,
From whose avenging penons fall
Thunder and Lightning twisted Spun;
Brave Cousin-german to the Sun!
That didst forsake thy Throne and Sphere,
To be an humble Pris'ner here;
And for a pirch of her soft hand,
Resign the Royal Woods command.

    How often would'st thou shoot Heav'ns Ark,
Then mount thy self into a Lark;
And after our short faint eyes call,
When now a Fly, now nought at all;
Then stoop so swift unto our Sence,
As thou wert sent Intelligence!

    Free beauteous Slave, thy happy feet
In silver Fetters vervails meet,
And trample on that noble Wrist
The Gods have kneel'd in vain t' have kist:
But gaze not, bold deceived Spye,
Too much oth' lustre of her Eye;
The Sun thou dost out-stare, alas!
Winks at the glory of her Face.

Be safe then in thy velvet helm,
Her looks are calms that do orewhelm,
Then the *Arabian* bird more blest,
Chafe in the spicery of her breast,
And loose you in her Breath a wind
Sow'rs the delicious gales of *Inde*.

But now a quill from thine own Wing
I pluck, thy lofty fate to sing;
Whilst we behold the various fight,
With mingled pleasure and affright,
The humbler Hinds do fall to pray'r,
As when an Army's seen i' th' Air,
And the prophetick Spannels run,
And howle thy *Epicedium*.

The *Heron* mounted doth appear
On his own Peg'sus a Lanceer,
And seems, on earth when he doth hut,
A proper Halberdier on foot;
Secure i' th' Moore, about to sup,
The Dogs have beat his Quarters up.

And now he takes the open air,
Drawes up his Wings with Tactick care;
Whilst th' expert *Falcon* swift doth climbe,
In subtle Mazes serpentine;
And to advantage closely twin'd
She gets the upper Sky and Wind,
Where she dissembles to invade,
And lies a pol'tick Ambuscade.

The hedg'd-in *Heron*, whom the Foe
Awaits above, and Dogs below,
In his fortification lies,
And makes him ready for surprize;
When roused with a shrill alarm,
Was shouted from beneath, they arm.

    The *Falcon* charges at first view
With her brigade of Talons; through
Whose Shoots, the wary *Heron* beat,
With a well counterwheel'd retreat.
But the bold Gen'ral never lost,
Hath won again her airy Post;
Who wild in this affront, now fryes,
Then gives a Volley of her Eyes.

    The desp'rate *Heron* now contracts,
In one design all former facts;
Noble he is resolv'd to fall
His, and his En'mies funerall,
And (to be rid of her) to dy
A publick Martyr of the Sky.

    When now he turns his last to wreak
The Palizadoes of his Beak;
The raging foe impatient
Wrack'd with revenge, and fury rent,
Swift as the Thunderbolt he strikes,
Too sure upon the stand of Pikes,
There she his naked breast doth hit,
And on the case of Rapiers's split.

    But ev'n in her expiring pangs
The *Heron*'s pounc'd within her Phangs,
And so above she stoops to rise
A Trophee and a Sacrifice;
Whilst her own Bells in the sad fall
Ring out the double Funerall.

    Ah, Victory, unhap'ly wonne!
Weeping and Red is set the Sun,
Whilst the whole Field floats in one tear,
And all the Air doth mourning wear:
Close hooded all thy kindred come

To pay their Vows upon thy Tombe;
The *Hobby* and the *Musket* too,
Do march to take their last adieu.

  The *Lanner* and the *Lanneret*,
Thy Colours bear as Banneret;
The *Goshawk* and her *Tercel* rows'd,
With Tears attend thee as new bows'd,
All these are in their dark array
Led by the various *Herald-Jay*.

  But thy eternal name shall live
Whilst Quills from Ashes fame reprieve,
Whilst open stands Renown's wide dore,
And Wings are left on which to soar;
Doctor *Robbin*, the Prelate *Pye*,
And the poetick *Swan*, shall dye,
Only to sing thy Elegie.

Love made in the first Age:
To Chloris

In the Nativity of time,
Chloris! it was not thought a Crime
  In direct *Hebrew* for to woe.
Now wee make Love, as all on fire,
Ring Retrograde our lowd Desire,
  And Court in *English* Backward too.

II.

Thrice happy was that golden Age,
When Complement was constru'd Rage,
  And fine words in the Center hid;
When cursed *No* stain'd no Maids Blisse,
And all discourse was summ'd in *Yes*,
  And Nought forbad, but to forbid.

III.

Love then unstinted, Love did sip,
And Cherries pluck'd fresh from the Lip,
    On Cheeks and Roses free he fed;
Lasses like *Autumne* Plums did drop,
And Lads, indifferently did crop
    A Flower, and a Maiden-head.

IV.

Then unconfined each did Tipple
Wine from the Bunch, Milk from the Nipple;
    Paps tractable as Udders were;
Then equally the wholsome Jellies,
Were squeez'd from Olive-Trees, and Bellies,
    Nor Suits of Trespasse did they fear.

V.

A fragrant Bank of Straw-berries,
Diaper'd with Violets Eyes,
    Was Table, Table-cloth, and Fare;
No Pallace to the Clouds did swell,
Each humble Princesse then did dwell
    In the *Piazza* of her hair.

VI.

Both broken faith and th' cause of it,
All-damning gold, was damn'd to th' pit;
    Their troth seal'd with a Clasp and Kisse,
Lasted untill that extreem day,
In which they smil'd their Souls away,
    And in each other breath'd new blisse.

VII.

Because no fault, there was no tear;
No grone did grate the granting Ear,
    No false foul breath, their Del'cat smell.
No Serpent kiss poyson'd the Tast,

Each touch was naturally Chast,
    And their mere Sense a Miracle.

VIII.

Naked as their own innocence,
And unimbroyder'd from Offence
    They went, above poor Riches, gay;
On softer than the Cignets Down,
In beds they tumbled off their own;
    For each within the other lay.

IX.

Thus did they live: Thus did they love,
Repeating only joyes Above;
    And Angels were, but with Cloaths on,
Which they would put off cheerfully,
To bathe them in the *Galaxie*,
    Then gird them with the Heavenly Zone.

X.

Now, *Chloris*! miserably crave
The offer'd blisse you would not have;
    Which evermore I must deny,
Whilst ravish'd with these Noble Dreams,
And crowned with mine own soft Beams,
    Injoying of my self I lye.

To a Lady with child that ask'd an Old Shirt

And why an honour'd ragged Shirt, that shows,
Like tatter'd Ensigns, all its Bodies blows?
Should it be swathed in a vest so dire,
It were enough to set the Child on fire;
Dishevell'd Queens should strip them of their hair,
And in it mantle the new rising Heir:

Nor do I know ought worth to wrap it in,
Except my parchment upper-coat of Skin;
And then expect no end of its chast Tears,
That first was rowl'd in Down, now Furs of Bears.

   But since to Ladies 't hath a Custome been
Linnen to send, that travail and lye in;
To the nine Sempstresses, my former friends,
I su'd; but they had nought but shreds and ends.
At last, the jolli'st of the three times three
Rent th' apron from her smock, and gave it me;
'Twas soft and gentle, subt'ly spun, no doubt;
Pardon my boldness, Madam; *Here's the clout.*

SONG

I.

In mine one Monument I lye,
   And in my Self am buried;
Sure the quick Lightning of her Eye
   Melted my soul ith' Scabberd, dead;
And now like some pale ghost I walk,
And with anothers Spirit talk.

II.

Nor can her beams a heat convey
   That may my frozen bosome warm,
Unless her Smiles have pow'r, as they
   That a cross charm can countercharm;
But this is such a pleasing pain,
I'm loth to be alive again.

Another

I did believe I was in Heav'n
When first the Heav'n her self was giv'n,
That in my heart her beams did passe
As some the Sun keep in a glasse,
So that her Beauties thorow me
Did hurt my Rival-Enemy.
But fate, alas! decreed it so,
That I was Engine to my woe;
For, as a corner'd Christal Spot
My heart Diaphanous was not;
But solid Stuffe, where her Eye flings
Quick fire upon the catching strings:
Yet as at Triumphs in the Night,
You see the Princes Arms in Light;
So, when I once was set on flame,
I burnt all ore the Letters of her Name.

ODE

1.

You are deceiv'd; I sooner may dull fair,
Seat a dark *Moor* in *Cassiopea*'s chair,
  Or on the Glow-worm's uselesse Light
  Bestow the watching flames of Night,
     Or give the Roses breath
      To executed Death,
        Ere the bright hiew
        Of Verse to you;
It is just Heaven on Beauty stamps a fame,
And we, alas! its Triumphs but proclaim.

II.

What chains but are too light for me, should I
Say that *Lucasta*, in strange Arms could lie;
  Or that *Castara* were impure,
  Or *Saccarisa*'s faith unsure;
     That *Chloris*' Love, as hair,
     Embrac'd each En'mies air:
        That all their good
        Ran in their blood;
'Tis the same wrong th' unworthy to inthrone,
As from her proper sphere t' have vertue thrown.

III.

That strange force on the ignoble hath renown,
As *Aurum Fulminans*, it blows Vice down;
  'Twere better (heavy one) to crawl
  Forgot, then raised, trod on fall;
     All your defections now
     Are not writ on your brow.
        Odes to faults give
        A shame, must live.
When a fat mist we view, we coughing run;
But that once Meteor drawn, all cry, undone.

IV.

How bright the fair *Paulina* did appear,
When hid in Jewels she did seem a Star:
  But who could soberly behold
  A wicked Owl in Cloath of Gold?
     Or the ridiculous *Ape*,
     In sacred *Vesta*'s Shape?
        So doth agree
        Just Praise with thee;
For since thy birth gave thee no beauty, know
No Poets pencil must or can do so.

The Duell

L ove drunk the other day, knockt at my brest,
    But I, alas! was not within:
My man, my Ear, told me he came t' attest,
    That without cause h' had boxed him,
And battered the Windows of mine eyes,
And took my heart for one of 's Nunneries.

II.
I wondred at the outrage safe return'd,
    And stormed at the base affront;
And by a friend of mine, bold Faith, that burn'd,
    I called him to a strict Accompt.
He said, that by the Law, the challeng'd might
Take the advantage both of Arms, and Fight.

III.
Two darts of equal length and points he sent,
    And nobly gave the choyce to me;
Which I not weigh'd, young and indifferent;
    Now full of nought but Victorie.
So we both met in one of 's Mothers Groves,
The time, at the first murm'ring of her Doves.

IV.
I stript myself naked all o're, as he,
    For so I was best arm'd, when bare;
His first pass did my Liver rase, yet I
    Made home a falsify too neer;
For when my Arm to its true distance came,
I nothing touch'd but a fantastick flame.

V.
This, this is Love we daily quarrel so,
    An idle *Don-Quichoterie*:
We whip our selves with our own twisted wo,
    And wound the Ayre for a Fly.

The only way t' undo this Enemy
Is to laugh at the Boy, and he will cry.

Cupid *far gone*

What, so beyond all madnesse is the Elf,
    Now he hath got out of himself!
  His fatal Enemy the *Bee*,
  Nor his deceiv'd Artillerie;
  His Shackles, nor the Roses bough
Ne'r half so netled him, as he is now.

II.
See! at's own Mother he is offering;
  His Finger now fits any Ring;
  Old *Cybele* he would enjoy,
  And now the Girl, and now the Boy.
  He proffers *Jove* a back caresse,
And all his Love in the *Antipodes*.

III.
Jealous of his chast *Psyche*, raging he,
  Quarrels with Student *Mercurie*;
  And with a proud submissive Breath
  Offers to change his Darts with Death.
  He strikes at the bright Eye of Day,
And *Juno* tumbles in her milky way.

IV.
The dear Sweet Secrets of the Gods he tells,
  And with loath'd hate lov'd heaven he swells;
  Now, like a fury, he belies
  Myriads of pure Virginities;
  And swears, with this false frenzy hurl'd,
There's not a vertuous She in all the World.

V.

Olympus he renownces, then descends,
    And makes a friendship with the Fiends;
    Bids *Charon* be no more a slave,
    He *Argos* rigg'd with Stars shall have;
    And triple *Cerberus* from below
Must leash'd t' himself with him a hunting go.

A Mock-Song

Now *Whitehall's* in the grave,
    And our *Head* is our slave,
The bright pearl in his close shell of Oyster;
    Now the *Miter* is lost,
    The proud *Prælates*, too, crost
And all *Rome's* confined to a Cloyster:
    He that *Tarquin* was styl'd,
    Our white Land's exil'd,
        Yea undefil'd,
Not a Court *Ape's* left to confute us:
    Then let your Voyces rise high,
    As your Colours did fly,
        And flour'shing cry,
Long live the brave *Oliver-Brutus*.

    Now the *Sun* is unarm'd,
    And the *Moon* by us charm'd,
All the *Stars* dissolv'd to a Jelly;
    Now the *Thighs* of the Crown,
    And the *Arms* are lopp'd down,
And the *Body* is all but a Belly:
    Let the *Commons* go on,
    The Town is our own,
        We'll rule alone;
For the *Knights* have yielded their Spent-gorge;

And an order is tane,
   With *HONY SOIT* profane,
      Shout forth amain,
For our Dragon hath vanquished the St. *George*.

A Fly caught in a Cobweb

Small type of great ones, that do hum,
Within this whole World's narrow Room,
That with a busie hollow Noise
Catch at the people's vainer Voice,
And with spread Sails play with their breath,
Whose very Hails new christen Death.
Poor Fly, caught in an airy net,
Thy Wings have fetter'd now thy feet;
Where, like a *Lyon* in a Toyl,
Howere, thou keep'st a noble Coyl,
And beat'st thy gen'rous breast, that ore
The plains thy fatal buzzes rore,
Till thy all-belly'd foe (round Elf)
Hath quarter'd thee within himself.
    Was it not better once to play
I' th' light of a Majestick Ray?
Where though too neer and bold, the fire
Might sindge thy upper down attire,
And thou ith' storm to loose an Eye,
A Wing, or a self-trapping Thigh;
Yet hadst thou fal'n like him, whose Coil
Made Fishes in the Sea to broyl;
When now th'ast scap'd the noble Flame,
Trapp'd basely in a slimy frame;
And free of Air, thou art become
Slave to the spawn of Mud and Lome?
    Nor is't enough thy self do'st dresse
To thy swoln Lord a num'rous messe,

And by degrees thy thin Veins bleed,
And piecemeal dost his poyson feed;
But now devour'd, art like to be
A Net spun for thy Familie,
And, straight expanded in the Air
Hang'st for thy issue too a snare.
Strange witty Death, and cruel ill,
That killing thee, thou thine dost kill!
Like Pies, in whose intombed ark,
All Fowl crowd downward to a Lark;
Thou art thine En'mies Sepulcher,
And in thee buriest, too, thine heir.
    Yet Fates a glory have reserv'd
For one so highly hath deserv'd;
As the *Rhinoceros* doth dy
Under his Castle-Enemy,
As through the *Cranes* trunk Throat doth speed,
The *Aspe* doth on his feeder feed;
Fall yet triumphant in thy woe,
Bound with the entrails of thy foe.

A Fly about a Glasse of Burnt Claret

I.

Forbear this liquid Fire, *Fly*,
It is more fatal then the dry,
That singly, but embracing, wounds,
And this at once, both burns and drowns.

II.

The Salamander that in heat
And flames doth cool his monstrous sweat;
Whose fan a glowing cake, 'tis said,
Of this red furnace is afraid.

III.
Viewing the Ruby-christal shine,
Thou tak'st it for Heaven-Christalline;
Anon thou wilt be taught to groan,
'Tis an ascended *Acheron*.

IV.
A Snowball-heart in it let fall,
And take it out a Fire-ball;
An Icy breast in it betray'd,
Breaks a destructive wild Granade.

V.
'Tis this makes *Venus* Altars shine,
This kindles frosty *Hymen*'s Pine;
When the Boy grows old in his desires,
This *Flambeau* doth new light his fires.

VI.
'Though the cold *Hermit* ever wail,
Whose sighs do freeze, and tears drop hail,
Once having pass'd this, will ne'r
Another flaming purging fear.

VII.
The *Vestal* drinking this doth burn
Now more than in her fun'ral Urn;
Her fires, that with the Sun kept race,
Are now extinguish'd by her Face.

VIII.
The *Chymist*, that himself doth still,
Let him but tast this *Limbecks* bill,
And prove this sublimated Bowl,
He'll swear it will calcine a Soul.

IX.

Noble, and brave! now thou dost know,
The false prepared decks below,
Dost thou the fatal liquor sup,
One drop, alas! thy Barque blowes up.

X.

What airy Country hast to save,
Whose plagues thou'lt bury in thy grave?
For even now thou seem'st to us
On this Gulphs brink a *Curtius*.

XI.

And now th' art fall'n (magnanimous *Fly*)
In, where thine Ocean doth fry,
Like the Sun's son who blush'd the flood,
To a complexion of blood.

XII.

Yet see! my glad Auricular
Redeems thee (though dissolv'd) a Star,
Flaggy thy Wings, and scorch'd thy Thighs,
Thou ly'st a double Sacrifice.

XIII.

And now my warming, cooling, breath
Shall a new life afford in Death;
See! in the Hospital of my hand
Already cur'd, thou fierce do'st stand.

XIV.

Burnt Insect! dost thou reaspire
The moist-hot-glasse, and liquid fire?
I see! 'tis such a pleasing pain,
Thou wouldst be scorch'd, and drown'd again!

Female Glory

'Mongst the worlds wonders, there doth yet remain
One greater than the rest, that's all those o're again,
And her own self beside: A *Lady*, whose soft Breast,
Is with vast Honours Soul and Virtues Life possest.
Fair, as Original Light, first from the *Chaos* shot,
When day in Virgin-beams triumph'd, and Night was not,
And as that Breath infus'd, in the New-breather Good,
When Ill unknown was dumb, and Bad not understood;
Chearful, as that Aspect at this world's finishing,
When Cherubims clapp'd wings, and th' Sons of Heaven did sing.
Chast as th' *Arabian* bird, who all the Ayr denyes,
And ev'n in Flames expires, when with her selfe she lyes.
Oh! she's as *kind* as drops of new faln *April* Showers,
That on each gentle breast, spring fresh perfuming flowers;
She's *Constant, Gen'rous, Fixt*, she's *Calm*, she is the *All*
We can of *Vertue, Honour, Faith*, or *Glory* Call,
And she is (whom I thus transmit to endless fame)
Mistresse oth' World, and me, and *LAURA* is her Name.

A Dialogue
Lute *and* Voice

L. Sing, *Laura*, sing, whilst silent are the Sphears,
   And all the eyes of Heaven are turn'd to ears.

V. Touch thy dead Wood, and make each living tree,
   Unchain its feet, take arms, and follow thee.

Chorus.
L. Sing. V. Touch. O Touch. L. O Sing,
Both. It is the Souls, Souls Sole offering.

V. Touch the Divinity of thy Chords, and make
   Each Heart string tremble, and each Sinew shake.

L. Whilst with your Voyce you Rarifie the Air,
   None but an host of Angels hover here.

   Chorus. Sing, Touch, &c.

V. Touch thy soft Lute, and in each gentle thread,
   The *Lyon* and the *Panther* captive lead.

L. Sing, and in Heav'n Inthrone deposed Love,
   Whilst Angels dance, and Fiends in order move.

   Double Chorus.
What sacred Charm may this then be
         In Harmonie,
That thus can make the Angels wild,
         The Devils mild,
And teach low Hell to Heav'n to swell,
And the High Heav'n to stoop to Hell?

A Mock Charon

DIALOGUE

Cha.   W.

W. Charon! Thou Slave! Thou Fool! Thou Cavaleer!
Cha. A Slave, a Fool, What Traitors voice I Hear?
W. Come bring thy Boat. Ch. No, sir. W. No sirrah why?
Cha. The Blest will disagree, and Fiends will mutiny
    At thy, at thy, unnumbred Treachery.
W. Villain, I have a Pass, which who disdains,
    I will sequester the *Elizian* plains.
Cha. Woes me! Ye gentle shades! where shall I dwell?
    He's come! It is not safe to be in Hell.

Chorus.
Thus man, his Honor lost, falls on these Shelves;
Furies and Fiends are still true to themselves.

Cha. You must, lost Fool, come in. **W.** Oh let me in!
But now I fear thy Boat will sink with my ore-weighty sin.
Where, courteous *Charon*, am I now? **Cha.** Vile rant!
At the gates of thy supreme Judge *Rhadamant*.

Double Chorus of Divels.
Welcome to Rape, to Theft, to Perjurie,
To all the ills thou wert, we cannot hope to be;
Oh, pitty us condemned! Oh cease to wooe,
And softly, softly breath, least you infect us too.

The Toad *and* Spyder
A *Duell*

Upon a Day, when the Dog-star
Unto the World proclaim'd a War,
And poyson bark'd from his black Throat,
And from his jaws Infection shot,
Under a deadly Hen-bane shade
With slime infernal Mists are made;
Met the two dreaded Enemies,
Having their Weapons in their eyes.
    First from his Den rolls forth that Load
Of Spite and Hate, the speckl'd Toad,
And from his Chaps a foam doth spawn,
Such as the loathed three Heads yawn;
Defies his foe with a fell Spet,
To wade through Death to meet with it;
Then in his self the *Lymbeck* turns,
And his Elixir'd poyson Urns.
Arachne once the fear oth' Maid

Cœlestial, thus unto her pray'd:
Heaven's blew-ey'd Daughter, thine own Mother!
The *Python*-killing Sun's thy Brother.
Oh! thou from gods that did'st descend,
With a poor Virgin to contend,
Shall seed of Earth and Hell ere be
A Rival in thy Victorie?
Pallas assents: for now long time
And pity, had clean rins'd her crime;
When straight she doth with active fire,
Her many legged foe inspire.
Have you not seen a Charact lie
A great Cathedral in the Sea,
Under whose *Babylonian* Walls
A small thin frigot-Alms-house stalls;
So in his slime the Toad doth float,
And th' Spyder by, but seems his Boat;
And now the Naumachie Begins
Close to the Surface, her self spins
Arachne, when her foe lets flye
A broad-side of his Breath, too high,
That's over-shot, the wisely stout
Advised Maid doth tack about,
And now her pitchy barque doth sweat,
Chaf'd in her own black fury wet;
Lasie and cold before, she brings
New fires to her contracted Stings,
And with discolour'd Spumes doth blast
The Herbs that to their Center hast.
Now to the Neighb'ring Henbane top
Arachne hath her self wound up,
And thence, from its dilated Leaves,
By her own cordage downwards weaves;
And doth her Town of Foe Attack,
And storms the Rampiers of his Back;
Which taken in her Colours spread,
March to th' Citadel of's Head.

Now as in witty torturing *Spain*,
The Brain is vext, to vex the Brain;
Where *Hereticks* bare Heads are arm'd
In a close Helm, and in it charm'd
An overgrown and Meagre Rat,
That Peece-meal nibbles himself fat;
So on the *Toads* blew-checquer'd Scull
The *Spider* gluttons her self full,
And Vomiting her *Stygian* Seeds,
Her poyson, on his poyson, feeds:
Thus the invenom'd Toad, now grown
Big, with more poyson than his own,
Doth gather all his pow'rs, and shakes
His Stormer in's Disgorged Lakes;
And wounded now, apace crawls on
To his next Plantane Surgeon;
With whose rich Balm no sooner drest,
But purged, is his sick swoln Breast;
And as a glorious Combatant,
That only rests awhile to pant;
Then with repeated strength, and Scars,
That smarting, fire him new to Wars,
Deals Blows that thick themselves prevent,
As they would gain the time he spent.
    So the disdaining angry Toad,
That, calls but a thin useless Load;
His fatal feared self comes back
With unknown Venome fill'd to crack.
Th' amased *Spider* now untwin'd,
Hath crept up, and her self new lin'd
With fresh salt foams, and Mists that blast
The Ambient Air as they past.
And now me thinks a *Sphynx*'s wing
I pluck, and do not write, but sting;
With their black blood, my pale inks blent,
Gall's but a faint Ingredient.
The Pol'tick *Toad* doth now withdraw,

Warn'd, higher in *Campania*.
There wisely doth intrenched deep,
His Body, in a Body keep,
And leaves a wide and open pass
T' invite the foe up to his jaws;
Which there within a foggy blind
With fourscore fire-arms were lin'd;
The gen'rous active *Spider* doubts
More Ambuscadoes, then Redoubts;
So within shot she doth pickear,
Now gall's the Flank, and now the Rear;
As that the *Toad* in's own dispite
Must change the manner of his fight,
Who like a glorious General,
With one home Charge, lets fly at All.
Chaf'd with a fourfold ven'mous Foam
Of Scorn, Revenge, his Foes and 's Own;
He seats him in his loathed Chair,
New-made him by each Mornings Air;
With glowing Eyes, he doth survey
Th' undaunted hoast, he calls his prey;
Then his dark Spume he gred'ly laps,
And shows the foe his Grave, his Chaps.
    Whilst the quick wary Amazon
Of 'vantage takes occasion,
And with her troop of Leggs Carreers,
In a full speed with all her Speers;
Down (as some mountain on a Mouse)
On her small Cot he flings his house;
Without the poyson of the Elf,
The *Toad* had like t' have burst himself,
For sage *Arachne* with good heed,
Had stopt herself upon full speed;
And 's body now disorder'd, on
She falls to Execution.
The passive *Toad* now only can
Contemn, and suffer: Here began

The wronged Maids ingenious Rage,
Which his heart venome must Asswage;
One Eye she hath spet out, strange Smother!
When one flame doth put out Another,
And one Eye wittily spar'd, that he
Might but behold his miserie;
She on each spot a wound doth print,
And each speck hath a sting within't;
Till he but one new Blister is,
And swells his own Periphrasis;
Then fainting, sick, and yellow, pale,
She baths him with her sulph'rous Stale;
Thus slacked is her *Stygian* fire,
And she vouchsafes now to retire;
Anon the *Toad* begins to pant,
Bethinks him of th' Almighty plant,
And lest he peece-meal should be sped,
Wisely doth finish himself dead.
Whilst the gay Girl, as was her fate,
Doth wanton and luxuriate,
And crowns her conqu'ring head all ore
With fatall leaves of *Hellebore*,
Not guessing at the pretious Aid
Was lent her by the heavenly Maid.
The neer expiring *Toad* now rowls
Himself in lazy bloody Scrowls,
To th' sov'raign salve of all his ills,
That only life and health distills.
But loe! a Terror above all,
That ever yet did him befall!
    Pallas still mindful of her foe,
(Whilst they did with each fires glow)
Had to the place the *Spiders Lar*,
Dispatch'd before the Ev'nings Star;
He learned was in Natures Laws,
Of all her foliage knew the cause,
And 'mongst the rest in his choice want

Unplanted had this Plantane plant.
    The all-confounded *Toad* doth see
His life fled with his Remedie,
And in a glorious Despair
First burst himself, and next the Air;
Then with a Dismal Horred yell
Beats down his loathsome Breath to Hell.
    But what inestimable bliss
This to the sated Virgin is,
Who as before of her fiend foe,
Now full is of her Goddess too;
She from her fertile womb hath spun
Her stateliest Pavillion,
Whilst all her silken Flags display,
And her triumphant Banners play;
Where *Pallas* she ith' midst doth praise,
And counterfeits her Brothers Rayes;
Nor will she her dear *Lar* forget,
Victorious by his Benefit;
Whose Roof inchanted she doth free,
From haunting Gnat, and goblin Bee,
Who trapp'd in her prepared Toyle,
To their destruction keep a coyle.
    Then she unlocks the *Toad*'s dire head,
Within whose cell is treasured
That pretious stone, which she doth call
A noble recompence for all,
And to her *Lar* doth it present,
Of his fair Aid a Monument.

The *Triumphs* of PHILAMORE and AMORET

To The Noblest of our Youth And Best of Friends, *CHARLES COTTON*, Esquire. Being at *Berisford*, at his house in Staffordshire. From *LONDON*.

A *Poem*

Sir, your sad absence I complain, as Earth
Her long hid Spring, that gave her verdures birth,
Who now her cheerful Aromatick Head
Shrinks in her *cold* and *dismal* widow'd *bed*;
Whilst the false Sun her Lover doth him move
Below, and to th' *Antipodes* make Love.
    What Fate was mine, when in mine obscure Cave
(Shut up almost close Prisoner in a Grave)
Your Beams could reach me through this Vault of Night,
And Canton the dark Dungeon with Light!
Whence me (as gen'rous *Spahy's*) you unbound,
Whilst I now know my self both *Free* and Crown'd.
    But as at *Mæcha's* tombe, the Devout blind
Pilgrim (great Husband of his Sight and Mind)
Pays to no other Object this chast prise,
Then with hot Earth anoynts out both his Eyes:
So having seen your dazling Glories store;
It is enough, and sin for to see more?
    Or, do you thus those pretious Rayes withdraw
To whet my dull Beams, keep my Bold in aw?
Or, are you gentle and compassionate,
You will not reach me *Regulus* his Fate?
Brave Prince who Eagle-ey'd of Eagle kind,
Wert blindly damn'd to look thine own self blind!
    But oh return those Fires, too Cruel Nice!
For whilst you fear me Cindars, See! I'm Ice;
A nummed speaking clod, and mine own show,

My Self congeal'd, a Man cut out in Snow:
Return those living Fires, Thou who that vast
Double advantage from one-ey'd Heav'n hast;
Look with one *Sun*, though 't but Obliquely be,
And if not shine, vouchsafe to wink on me.

 Perceive you not a gentle, gliding heat,
And quick'ning warmth, that makes the *Statua* sweat;
As rev'rend *Ducaleon*'s back-flung stone,
Whose rough out-side softens to Skin, anon
Each crusty Vein with wet red is suppli'd,
Whilst nought of Stone but in its heart doth 'bide.

 So from the rugged North, where your soft stay
Hath stampt them a *Meridian*, and kind day;
Where now each *a la Mode* Inhabitant
Himself and 's Manners both do pay you rent,
And 'bout your house (your Pallace) doth resort
And 'spite of Fate and War creates a court.

 So from the taught North, when you shall return
To glad those Looks that ever since did mourn,
When men uncloathed of themselves you'l see,
Then start new made, fit, what they ought to be;
Hast! hast! you, that your Eyes on rare Sights feed,
For thus the golden *Triumph* is decreed.

 The twice-born God, still gay and ever young,
With Ivie crown'd, first leads the glorious Throng:
He *Ariadnes* starry Coronet
Designs for th' brighter Beams of *Amoret*;
Then doth he broach his Throne, and singing quaff
Unto her Health his pipe of God-head off.

 Him follow the recanting, vexing Nine
Who, wise, now sing thy lasting Fame in Wine;
Whilst *Phœbus*, not from th' East, your Feast t'adorn,
But from th' inspir'd *Canaries* rose this morn.

 Now you are come, Winds in their Caverns sit,
And nothing breaths, but new inlarged Wit;
Hark! One proclaims it *Piacle* to be sad,
And th' people call't *Religion* to be Mad.

    But now, as at a Coronation,
When noyse, the guard, and trumpets are oreblown,
The silent Commons mark their Princes way,
And with still Reverence both look, and pray;
So they amaz'd, expecting do adore,
And count the rest but *Pageantry* before.
    Behold! an Hoast of Virgins, pure as th' Air,
In her first face, ere Mists durst vayl her hair;
Their snowy Vests, White as their whiter Skin,
Or their far chaster whiter Thoughts within:
Roses they breath'd and strew'd, as if the fine
Heaven, did to Earth his Wreath of sweets resigne;
They sang aloud! *Thrice, oh Thrice happy They*
That can like these in Love both yield and sway.
    Next Herald Fame (a Purple Clowd her bears)
In an imbroider'd Coat of Eyes and Ears,
Proclaims the Triumph, and these Lovers glory;
Then in a book of Steel Records the Story.
    And now a Youth of more than God-like form,
Did th'inward minds of the dumb Throng Alarm;
All nak'd, each part betray'd unto the Eye,
Chastly, for neither Sex ow'd he or she.
And this was Heav'nly Love; by his bright hand,
A Boy of worse than earthly stuffe did stand;
His Bow broke, his Fires out, and his Wings clipt,
And the black Slave from all his false flames stript;
Whose Eyes were new restor'd, but to confesse
This day's bright blisse, and his own wretchednesse;
Who swell'd with envy, bursting with disdain,
Did cry to cry, and weep them out again.
    And now what Heav'n must I invade, what Sphere
Rifle of all her Stars t' inthrone her there?
No *Phoebus*, by thy Boys fate we beware,
Th' unruly flames oth' firebrand, thy Carr;
Although she there once plac'd, thou *Sun* shouldst see
Thy day both Nobler governed and thee.
Drive on Boötes thy cold heavy wayn,

Then grease thy Wheels with Amber in the Main,
And *Neptune*, thou to thy false *Thetis* gallop,
Appollo's set within thy Bed of Scallop:
Whilst *Amoret* on the reconciled Winds
Mounted, is drawn by six Cælestial Minds;
She armed was with Innocence, and fire
That did not burn, for it was *Chast Desire*;
Whilst a new Light doth gild the standers by;
Behold! it was a Day shot from her Eye;
Chafing perfumes oth' East did throng and sweat,
But by her breath, they melting back were beat.
A Crown of Yet-nere-lighted stars she wore,
In her soft hand a bleeding Heart she bore,
And round her lay Millions of broken more;
Then a wing'd Crier thrice aloud did call,
Let Fame proclaim this one great Prise for all.

  By her a Lady that might be call'd fair,
And justly, but that *Amoret* was there,
Was Pris'ner led; th' unvalewed Robe she wore,
Made infinite Lay Lovers to adore,
Who vainly tempt her Rescue (madly bold)
Chained in sixteen thousand links of gold;
Chrysetta thus (Loaden with treasures) Slave
Did strow the pass with Pearls, and her way pave.

  But loe! the glorious Cause of all this high
True heav'nly state, Brave *Philamore* draws nigh!
Who not himself, more seems himself to be,
And with a sacred Extasie doth see;
Fixt and unmov'd on's *Pillars* he doth stay,
And Joy transforms him his own *Statua*;
Nor hath he pow'r to breath, or strength to greet
The gentle Offers of his *Amoret*,
Who now amaz'd at 's noble Breast doth knock,
And with a Kiss his gen'rous heart unlock;
Whilst she and the whole pomp doth enter there,
Whence Her nor *Time* nor *Fate* shall ever tear.
But whether am I hurld? ho! Back! Awake

From thy glad Trance; to thine old Sorrow take!
Thus, after view of all the *Indies* store,
The Slave returns unto his Chain and Oar;
Thus *Poets* who all Night in blest Heav'ns dwell,
Are call'd next morn to their true living *Hell*;
So I unthrifty, to myself untrue,
Rise cloath'd with real wants, 'cause wanting you,
And what substantial Riches I possesse,
I must to these unvalued Dreams confesse.

  But all our Clowds shall be oreblown, when thee
In our Horizon, bright, once more we see;
When thy dear presence shall our Souls new dress,
And spring an universal cheerfulnesse;
When we shall be orewhelm'd in Joy, like they
That change their Night, for a vast half-years day.

  Then shall the wretched Few, that do repine,
See; and recant their Blasphemies in Wine;
Then shall they grieve, that thought I've sung to free
High and aloud of thy true worth and Thee,
And their fowl Heresies and Lips submit
To th' all-forgiving Breath of *Amoret*;
And me alone their angers Object call,
That from my height so miserably did fall;
And crie out my Invention thin and poor,
Who have said nought, since I could say no more.

Advice to my Best Brother,
Coll: Francis Lovelace

F*Rank*, wil't live handsomely? trust not too far
 Thy self to waving Seas: for what thy star
Calculated by sure event, must be,
Look in the Glassy-epithete, and see.

  Yet settle here your rest, and take your state,
And in calm *Halcyon*'s nest ev'n build your Fate;

Prethee lye down securely, *Frank*, and keep
With as much no noyse the inconstant Deep
As its Inhabitants; nay stedfast stand,
As if discover'd were a New-found-land,
Fit for Plantation here; dream, dream still,
Lull'd in *Dione*'s cradle, dream, untill
Horrour awake your sense, and you now find
Your self a bubbled pastime for the Wind,
And in loose *Thetis* blankets torn and tost;
Frank, to undo thy self why art at cost?

    Nor be too confident, fix'd on the shore,
For even that too borrows from the store
Of her rich Neighbour, since now wisest know,
(And this to *Galileo*'s judgement ow),
The palsie Earth it self is every jot
As frail, inconstant, waveing as that blot
We lay upon the Deep; That sometimes lies
Chang'd, you would think, with's botoms properties,
But this eternal strange *Ixion*'s wheel
Of giddy earth, ne'er whirling leaves to reel
Till all things are inverted, till they are
Turn'd to that Antick confus'd state they were.

    Who loves the golden mean, doth safely want
A cobwebb'd Cot, and wrongs entail'd upon't;
He richly needs a Pallace for to breed
Vipers and Moths, that on their feeder feed;
The toy that we (too true) a Mistress call,
Whose Looking-glass and feather weighs up all;
And Cloaths which Larks would play with, in the Sun,
That mock him in the Night, when's course is run.

    To rear an edifice by Art so high
That envy should not reach it with her eye,
Nay with a thought come neer it, would'st thou know
How such a Structure should be raised? build low.
The blust'ring winds invisible rough stroak,

More often shakes the stubborn'st, prop'rest Oak,
And in proud Turrets we behold withal,
'Tis the Imperial top declines to fall:
Nor does Heav'n's lightning strike the humble Vales
But high-aspiring Mounts batters and scales.

   A breast of proof defies all Shocks of Fate,
Fears in the best, hopes in worser state;
Heaven forbid that, as of old, Time ever
Flourish'd in *Spring* so contrary, now never:
That mighty breath which blew foul Winter hither,
Can eas'ly puffe it to a fairer weather.
Why dost despair then, *Franck*? *Æolus* has
A *Zephyrus* as well as *Boreas*.

   'Tis a false Sequel, Solœcisme, 'gainst those
Precepts by fortune giv'n us, to suppose
That 'cause it is now ill, 't will ere be so;
Apollo doth not always bend his Bow;
But oft uncrowned of his Beams divine,
With his soft harp awakes the sleeping Nine.

   In strictest things magnanimous appear,
Greater in hope, howere thy fate, then fear:
Draw all your Sails in quickly, though no storm
Threaten your ruine with a sad alarm;
For tell me how they differ, tell me pray,
A cloudy tempest, and a too fair day.

An Anniversary
On the Hymeneals of my Noble Kinsman
Tho. Stanley, *Esquire*

1.

The day is curl'd about agen
    To view the splendor she was in;
        When first with hallow'd hands
The holy man knit the mysterious bands;
When you two your contracted Souls did move,
    Like *Cherubims* above,
        And did make Love,
As your un-understanding issue now
In a glad sigh, a smile, a tear, a Vow.

2.

Tell me, O self-reviving Sun,
    In thy Perigrination,
        Hast thou beheld a pair
Twist their soft beams like these in their chast air;
As from bright numberlesse imbracing rayes
        Are sprung th' industrious dayes;
            So when they gaze,
And change their fertile Eyes with the new morn,
A beauteous Offspring is shot forth, not born.

3.

Be witness then, all-seeing Sun,
    Old Spy, thou that thy race hast run,
        In full five thousand Rings;
To thee were ever purer Offerings
Sent on the Wings of Faiths? and thou, oh Night!
        Curtain of their delight,
            By these made bright,
Have you not mark'd their Cœlestial play,
And no more peek'd the gayeties of day?

4.

Come then, pale Virgins, Roses strow,
　　Mingled with *Io*'s as you go;
　　　　The snowy Oxe is kill'd,
The fane with pros'lite Lads and Lasses fill'd,
You too may hope the same *seraphick* joy,
　　　　Old time cannot destroy,
　　　　　　Nor fulnesse cloy,
When like these, you shall stamp by Sympathies,
Thousands of new-born-loves with your chast eyes.

Paris's *Second Judgement*

Upon the three Daughters of my Dear Brother Mr. R. Caesar

Behold! three Sister-wonders, in whom met,
　　Distinct and chast, the Splendors counterfeit
Of *Juno, Venus* and the warlike Maid,
Each in their three Divinities array'd!
The Majesty and State of Heav'ns great Queen,
And when she treats the gods, her noble Meen;
The sweet victorious beauties, and desires
O' th' Sea-born Princess, Empresse too of Fires;
The sacred Arts, and glorious Lawrels, torn
From the fair brow o' th' Goddesse Father-born;
All these were quarter'd in each snowy coat,
With canton'd honours of their own, to boot:
Paris, by Fate new-wak'd from his dead Cell,
Is charg'd to give his doom impossible.
He views in each the brav'ry of all *Ide*;
Whilst one, as once three, doth his Soul divide.
Then sighs! so equally they're glorious all,
What pity the whole World is but one Ball.

Peinture

A Panegyrick to the Best Picture of Friendship,
Mr. Pet. Lilly

If *Pliny*, Lord High Treasurer of all
Natures exchequer shuffled in this our ball;
Pincture, her richer Rival, did admire,
And cry'd she wrought with more almighty fire,
That judg'd the unnumber'd issue of her Scrowl,
Infinite and various as her Mother Soul,
That contemplation into matter brought,
Body'd *Idæa's*, and could form a thought:
Why do I pause to couch the Cataract,
And the grosse pearls from our dull eyes abstract?
That, pow'rful *Lilly*, now awakened, we
This new Creation may behold by thee.
    To thy victorious pencil, all that Eyes
And minds call reach, do bow; the Deities
Bold *Poets* first but feign'd, you do, and make,
And from your awe they our Devotion take.
Your beauteous Pallet first defin'd Loves Queen,
And made her in her heav'nly colours seen;
You strung the Bow of the Bandite her Son,
And tipp'd his Arrowes with Religion.
Neptune, as unknown as his Fish might dwell,
But that you seat him in his throne of Shell.
The thunderers Artillery, and brand,
You fancied *Rome* in his fantastick hand.
And the pale frights, the pains and fears of Hell,
First from your sullen Melancholy fell.
Who cleft th' infernal Dog's loath'd head in three,
And spun out *Hydra*'s fifty necks? by thee
As prepossess'd w' enjoy th' *Elizian* plain,
Which but before was flatter'd in our brain.
Who ere yet view'd Airs child invisible,
A hollow Voice, but in thy subtile skill?
Faint stamm'ring *Eccho*, you so draw, that we

The very repercussion do see.
      Cheat *Hocus-pocus*-Nature an Essay
O' th' Spring affords us, *Praesto* and away;
You all the year do chain her, and her fruits,
Roots to their Beds, and flowers to their Roots.
Have not mine eyes feasted i' th' frozen *Zone*,
Upon a fresh new-grown Collation
Of Apples, unknown sweets, that seem'd to me
Hanging to tempt as on the fatal Tree;
So delicately limn'd I vow'd to try
My appetite impos'd upon my Eye?
      You Sir alone, Fame, and all-conqu'ring Rime,
Files the set teeth of all-devouring time.
When Beauty once thy vertuous paint hath on,
Age needs not call her to Vermilion;
Her Beams nere shed or change like th' hair of day,
She scatters fresh her everlasting Ray;
Nay, from her ashes her fair Virgin fire
Ascends, that doth new massacres conspire,
Whilst we wipe off the num'rous score of years,
And do behold our Grandsires as our peers,
With the first Father of our House, compare
We do the features of our new-born Heir;
For though each coppied a Son, they all
Meet in thy first and true Original.
      Sacred Luxurious! what Princesse not
But comes to you to have her self begot?
As when first man was kneaded, from his side
Is born to's hand a ready made up Bride.
He husband to his issue then doth play,
And for more Wives remove the obstructed way:
So by your Art you spring up in two moons
What could not else be form'd by fifteen Suns;
Thy Skill doth an'mate the prolifick flood,
And thy red Oyl assimilates to blood.
      Where then when all the world pays its respect,
Lies our transalpine barbarous Neglect?

When the chast hands of pow'rful *Titian*,
Had drawn the Scourges of our God and Man,
And now the top of th' Altar did ascend,
To crown the heav'nly piece with a bright end;
Whilst he who to seven Languages gave Law,
And always like the *Sun* his Subjects saw,
Did in his Robes Imperial and gold,
The basis of the doubtful Ladder hold.
O *Charls*! A nobler monument than that,
Which thou thine own Executor wert at.
When to our huffling *Henry* there complain'd
A grieved Earl, that thought his honor stain'd;
Away (frown'd he), for your own safeties, hast!
In one cheap hour ten Coronets I'l cast:
But *Holbeen*'s noble and prodigious worth,
Onely the pangs of an whole Age brings forth.
Henry! a word so princely saving said,
It might new raise the ruines thou hast made.
  O sacred *Peincture*! that dost fairly draw,
What but in Mists deep inward *Poets* saw;
'Twixt thee and an Intelligence no ods,
That art of privy Council to the Gods!
By thee unto our eyes they do prefer
A stamp of their abstracted Character;
Thou, that in frames eternity dost bind,
And art a written and a body'd mind;
To thee is Ope the *Juncto* o' th' Abysse,
And its conspiracy detected is;
Whilest their Cabal thou to our sense dost show,
And in thy square paint'st what they threat below.
  Now, my best *Lilly* let's walk hand in hand,
And smile at this un-understanding land;
Let them their own dull counterfeits adore,
Their Rainbow-cloaths admire, and no more;
Within one shade of thine more substance is
Than all their varnish'd Idol-Mistresses:
Whilst great *Vasari* and *Vermander* shall

Interpret the deep mystery of all,
And I unto our modern Picts shall show,
What due renown to thy fair Art they owe,
In the delineated lives of those,
By whom this everlasting Lawrel grows:
Then if they will not gently apprehend,
Let one great blot give to their fame an end;
Whilst no Poetick flower their Herse doth dresse,
But perish they and their Effigies.

To my Dear Friend Mr. E[ldred] R[evett] *On his Poems Moral and Divine*

Cleft as the top of the inspired Hill,
Struggles the Soul of my divided Quill,
Whilst this foot doth the watry mount aspire,
That *Sinai's* living and enlivening fire.
Behold my pow'rs storm'd by a twisted light
O' th' Sun, and his, first kindled his Sight,
And my left thoughts invoke the Prince of day,
My right to th' Spring of it and him do pray.
    Say, happy youth, crown'd with a heav'nly ray
Of the first Flame, and interwreathed bay,
Inform my Soul in Labour to begin,
Io's or *Anthems*, *Pæans* or a *Hymne*.
Shall I a Hecatombe on thy Tripod slay,
Or my devotions at thy Altar pay?
While which t' adore th' amaz'd World cannot tell,
The sublime Urim or deep Oracle.
    Heark how the moving chords temper our brain,
As when *Apollo* serenades the main,
Old *Ocean* smooths his sullen furrow'd front,
And *Nereids* do glide soft measures on't;
Whilst th'Air puts on its sleekest, smoothest face,
And each doth turn the others Looking-glasse;

So by the sinewy Lyre now strook we see
Into soft calms all storm of Poesie,
And former thundering and lightning Lines,
And Verse, now in its native lustre shines.

    How wert thou hid within thy self! how shut!
Thy pretious Iliads lock'd up in a Nut!
Not hearing of thee thou dost break out strong,
Invading forty thousand men in Song;
And we, secure in our thin empty heat,
Now find ourselves at once surpris'd and beat;
Whilst the most valiant of our Wits now sue,
Fling down their arms, ask Quarter too of you.

    So cabin'd up in its disguis'd course rust,
And Scurf'd all ore with its unseemly crust,
The Diamond, from 'midst the humbler stones,
Sparkling, shoots forth the price of Nations.

    Ye sage unridlers of the Stars, pray tell,
By what name shall I stamp my miracle?
Thou strange inverted *Æson*, that leap'st ore,
From thy first Infancy into fourscore,
That to thine own self hast the Midwife play'd,
And from thy brain spring'st forth the heav'nly maid!
Thou Staffe of him bore him, that bore our sins,
Which but set down, to bloom and bear begins.
Thou Rod of *Aaron* with one motion hurl'd,
Bud'st a perfume of Flowers through the World.
Thou strange calcined Seeds within a glass,
Each species *Idæa* spring'st as 't was;
Bright Vestal Flame, that kindled but ev'n now,
For ever dost thy sacred fires throw.

    Thus the repeated Acts of *Nestor*'s age,
That now had three times ore out-liv'd the Stage,
And all those beams contracted into one,
Alcides in his Cradle hath outdone.

    But all these flour'shing hiews, with which I dy
Thy Virgin Paper, now are vain as I;
For 'bove the Poets Heav'n th' art taught to shine,

And move, as in thy proper Christalline;
Whence that Mole-hill *Parnassus* thou dost view,
And us small *Ants* there dabbling in its dew;
Whence thy *Seraphick* Soul such Hymns doth play,
As those to which first danced the first day;
Where with a *thorn* from the *world-ransoming wreath*
Thou stung, dost *Antiphons* and *Anthems* breathe,
Where with an *Angels* quil dip'd i' th' *Lambs* blood,
Thou sing'st our *Pelicans* all-saving Flood,
And bath'st thy thoughts in everliving streams
Rench'd from Earth's tainted, fat, and heavy steams.
There move translated youth! inroll'd i' th' Quire,
That only doth with holy lays inspire;
To whom his burning Coach *Eliah* sent,
And th' royal Prophet-priest his Harp hath lent,
Which thou dost tune in consort, unto those
Clap Wings for ever at each hallow'd close;
Whilst we now weak and fainting in our praise,
Sick, Eccho ore thy *Halleluiahs*.

To my Noble Kinsman T[homas] S[tanley] Esq. *On his Lyrick* POEMS *composed by Mr.* J[ohn] G[amble]

1.

What means this stately Tablature,
    The Ballance of thy streins?
Which seems, in stead of sifting pure,
    T' extend and rack thy veins;
Thy *Odes* first their own Harmony did break,
For singing troth is but in tune to speak.

II.

Nor thus thy golden Feet and Wings,
    May it be thought false Melody

T' ascend to heav'n by silver strings,
    This is *Urania's* Heraldry:
Thy royal Poem now we may extol,
As truly *Luna* Blazon'd upon *Sol*.

III.

As when *Amphion* first did call
    Each listning stone from's Den;
And with the Lute did form his Wall,
    But with his words the men;
So in your twisted Numbers now, you thus,
Not only stocks perswade, but ravish us.

IV.

Thus do your Ayrs Eccho o're
    The Notes and *Anthems* of the *Sphæres*,
And their whole Consort back restore,
    As if Earth too would blesse Heav'ns Ears:
But yet the Spoaks by which they scal'd so high,
Gamble hath wisely laid of *Ut Re Mi*.

On the Best, last, and only remaining Comedy of Mr. Fletcher

The Wild Goose Chase

I'm un-ore-clowded too! free from the mist!
The *Blind* and late *Heavens-eyes* great *Occulist*,
Obscured with the *false fires* of His Sceme,
Not half those Souls are lightned by this Theme.
    Unhappy Murmurers, that still repine,
(After th' *Eclipse* our Sun doth brighter shine)
Recant your false grief and your true joys know,
Your blisse is endlesse, as you fear'd your Woe!
What fort'nate *Flood* is this? what *Storm* of Wit?

Oh who would *live* and not *ore-whelm'd* in it?
No more a *fatal Deluge* shall be hurl'd,
This *inundation* hath *sav'd* the world.
Once more the mighty *Fletcher* doth arise
Roab'd in a vest, studded with Stars and Eyes
Of all his former Glories; His last worth
Imbroiderd with what yet light ere brought forth.
See! in this glad farewel he doth appear
Stuck with the *Constellations* of his *Sphere*,
Fearing we Numm'd fear'd no Flagration,
Hath curled all his Fires in this one *One*;
Which (as they guard his hallowed chast Urn)
The dull aproaching Hereticks do burn.

    Fletcher at his adieu carouses thus,
To the Luxurious Ingenious;
As *Cleopatra* did of old out-vie,
Th' un-numb'red dishes of her *Anthony*,
When (he at th' empty board a wonderer)
Smiling she calls for Pearl and Vineger;
First pledges him in's *Breath*, then at one Draught
Swallows *Three Kingdomes* off *To his best Thought*.

    Hear, oh ye valiant Writers, and subscribe;
(His force set by) y' are conquer'd by this Bribe.
Though you *hold out your selves*, He doth commit
In this a sacred Treason on your wit:
Although in Poems desperately stout,
Give up; This Overture must *Buy you out*.

    Thus with some prodigal Us'rer 't doth fare,
That keeps his gold still *Vayl'd*, his Steel-breast *bare*;
That doth exclude his Coffers all but's *Eye*,
And his eyes Idol the *wing'd Deity*:
That cannot lock his *Mines* with half the Art
As some *rich* Beauty doth his *wretched Heart*;
Wild at his real Poverty, and so wise
To win her, turns himself into a *prise*.
First startles her with th' *Emerald Mad-lover*
The *Ruby Arcas*, least she should recover

Her dazled Thought a *Diamond* he throws,
Splendid in all the bright *Aspatia's* woes;
Then to sum up the Abstract of his store,
He flings a *rope* of *Pearl* of *forty* more.
Ah, see! the *stagg'ring Virtue faints*! which he
Beholding, darts his *Wealths Epitome*;
And now, to consummate her wished fall,
Shows this one *Carbuncle*, that *Darkens* all.

To Dr. F. Beale; **On his Book of** Chesse

Sir, now unravell'd is the Golden Fleece:
Men that could only fool at Fox and Geese,
Are new-made Polititians by thy Book,
And both can judge and conquer with a Look.
The hidden fate of Princes you unfold;
Court, Clergy, Commons, by your Law control'd;
    Strange, Serious Wantoning, all that they
      Bluster'd and clutter'd for, *you play.*

To the Genius of Mr. John Hall
33
On his exact Translation of Hierocles his Comment upon the golden Verses of Pythagoras

'Tis not from cheap thanks thinly to repay
  Th' Immortal Grove of thy fair-order'd bay,
Thou planted'st round my humble Fane, that I
Stick on thy Hearse this Sprig of *Elegie*:
Nor that your Soul so fast was link'd in me,
That now I've both since 't has forsaken thee:
That thus I stand a Swisse before thy gate,

And dare for such another time and fate.
Alas! our Faiths made different Essays,
Our *Minds* and *Merits* brake two several ways;
Justice commands, I wake thy learned Dust,
And truth, in whom all causes center must.

     Behold! when but a Youth, thou fierce didst whip
Upright the crooked Age, and gilt Vice strip;
A Senator *prætextat*, that knew'st to sway
The fasces, yet under the Ferula;
Rank'd with the Sage ere blossome did thy Chin,
Sleeked without, and Hair all ore within;
Who in the School could'st argue as in Schools,
Thy Lessons were ev'n Academie rules.
So that fair *Cam* saw thee matriculate,
At once a Tyro and a Graduate.

     At nineteen what *Essayes* have we beheld!
That well might have the Book of *Dogma*'s swell'd;
Tough *Paradoxes*, such as *Tully*'s, thou
Didst heat thee with, when snowy was thy Brow,
When thy undown'd face mov'd the Nine to shake,
And of the Muses did a Decad make;
What shall I say? by what Allusion bold?
None but the Sun was ere so young and old.

     Young reverend shade, ascend awhile! whilst we
Now celebrate this Posthume Victorie,
This Victory that doth contract in Death
Ev'n all the pow'rs and labours of thy breath;
Like the *Judean Hero*, in thy fall
Thou pull'st the house of Learning on us all.
And as that Soldier Conquest doubted not,
Who but one Splinter had of Castriot,
But would assault ev'n death so strongly charmd,
And naked oppose rocks, with his bone arm'd;
So we secure in this fair Relique stand,
The Slings and Darts shot by each profane Hand;
These Soveraign leaves thou left'st us are become
Sear clothes against all Times Infection.

Sacred *Hierocles*! whose heav'nly thought,
First acted ore this Comment, ere it wrought;
Thou hast so spirited, elixir'd, we
Conceive there is a noble Alchymie,
That's turning of this Gold, to something more
Pretious than Gold we never knew before.
Who now shall doubt the Metempsychosis,
Of the great Author, that shall peruse this?
Let others Dream thy shadow wandering strays
In th' *Elizian Mazes*, hid with bays;
Or that, snatcht up in th' upper Region,
'Tis kindled there a Constellation;
I have inform'd me, and Declare with ease,
Thy Soul is fled into Hierocles.

On Sanazar's *being honoured with six hundred Duckets by the* Clarissimi *of* Venice, *for composing an* Eligiack Hexastick *of* The City

A SATYRE

T'was a blith Prince exchang'd five hundred Crowns
For a fair Turnip; Dig, Dig on, O Clowns!
But how this comes about, *Fates* can you tell,
This more then Maid of Meurs, this miracle?
Let me not live, if I think not St. *Mark*
Has all the Oar, as well as Beasts in's Ark;
No wonder 'tis he marries the rich Sea,
But to betroth him to nak'd Poesie,
And with a bankrupt Muse to merchandise,
His treasures beams sure have put out his eyes.
His Conquest at *Lepanto* I'l let pass,
When the sick Sea with *Turbants* Night-cap'd was;
And now at *Candie* his full Courage shown,

That wain'd to a wan line the half-half Moon;
This is a wreath, this is a Victorie,
Cæsar himself would have look'd pale to see,
And in the height of all his Triumphs, feel
Himself but chain'd to such a mighty wheel.
    And now me thinks we ape *Augustus* state,
So ugly we his high worth imitate,
Monkey his Godlike glories; so that we
Keep light and form, with such deformitie,
As I have seen an arrogant Baboon
With a small piece of Glasse Zany the Sun.
    Rome to her Bard, who did her battails sing,
Indifferent gave to Poet and to King;
With the same Lawrells were his Temples fraught,
Who best had written, and who best had fought;
The Self same fame they equally did feel,
One's style ador'd as much as th' other's Steel.
A chain or fasces she could then afford
The sons of *Phœbus*, we an Axe, or Cord;
Sometimes a Coronet was her renown,
And ours the dear prerogative of a Crown.
In marble statu'd walks great *Lucan* lay,
And now we walk, our own pale *Statua*:
They the whole yeer with roses crownd would dine,
And we in all *December* know no wine;
Disciplin'd, dieted, sure there hath bin,
Ods 'twixt a Poet and a Capuchin.
    Of Princes, Women, Wine, to sing I see
Is no *Apocrypha*; for to rise high
Commend this Olio of this Lord, 'tis fit,
Nay ten to one but you have part of it;
There is that justice left, since you maintain
His table, he should counter-feed your brain.
Then write how well he in his Sack hath droll'd,
Straight there's a Bottle to your chamber roll'd,
Or with embroidered words praise his *French* Suit,
Month hence 'tis yours with his Mans curse to boot;

Or but applaud his boss'd Legs, two to none,
But he most nobly doth give you one:
Or spin an Elegie on his false hair,
'Tis well he cries, but living hair is dear;
Yet say that out of order ther's one curl,
And all the hopes of your reward you furl.
     Write a deep epick Poem, and you may
As soon delight them as the *Opera*,
Where they *Diogenes* thought in his Tub,
Never so sowre did look, so sweet a club.
     You that do suck for thirst your black quil's blood,
And chaw your labour'd papers for your food,
I will inform you how and what to praise,
Then skin y' in Satin as young *Lovelace* plaies.
Beware, as you would your fierce guests, your lice,
To strip the cloath of Gold from cherish'd vice;
Rather stand off with awe and reverend fear,
Hang a poetick pendant in her Ear.
Court her as her Adorers do their glass,
Though that as much of a true Substance has,
Whilst all the gall from your wild ink you drain,
The beauteous Sweets of Vertues Cheeks to stain;
And in your Livery let her be known,
As poor and tattered as in her own.
Nor write, nor speak you more of sacred writ,
But what shall force up your arrested wit.
Be chast Religion, and her Priests your scorn,
Whilst the vain Fanes of Idiots you adorn.
It is a mortal errour you must know,
Of any to speak good, if he be so.
Rayl till your edged breath flea your raw throat,
And burn all marks on all of gen'rous note;
Each verse be an inditement, be not free
Sanctity 't self from thy Scurrility.
Libel your Father, and your Dam *Buffoon*,
The Noblest Matrons of the Isle *Lampoon*,
Whilst *Aretine* and 's bodies you dispute,

And in your sheets your Sister prostitute.
    Yet there belongs a Sweetnesse, softnesse too,
Which you must pay, but first pray know to who.
There is a Creature, (if I may so call
That unto which they do all prostrate fall)
Term'd Mistress, when they'r angry, but pleas'd high,
It is a Princesse, Saint, Divinity.
To this they sacrifice the whole days light,
Then lye with their Devotion all night;
For this you are to dive to the Abysse,
And rob for Pearl the Closet of some Fish.
Arabia and *Sabæa* you must strip
Of all their Sweets, for to supply her Lip;
And steal new fire from Heav'n for to repair
Her unfledg'd Scalp with *Berenice*'s hair;
Then seat her in *Cassiopeia*'s Chair,
As now you're in your Coach. Save you bright Sir
(O spare your thanks) is not this finer far
Then walk un-hided, when that every Stone
Has knock'd acquaintance with your Anckle bone?
When your wing'd papers, like the last dove, nere
Return'd to quit you of your hope or fear,
But left you to the mercy of your Host,
And your days fare, a fortified Toast.
    How many battels sung in Epick strain,
Would have procur'd your head *thatch* from the *rain*?
Not all the arms of *Thebes* and *Troy* would get
One knife but to anatomize your meat,
A funeral Elegy with a sad boon
Might make you (*hei*) sip wine like Maccaroon;
But if perchance there did a Riband come,
Not the Train-band so fierce with all its drum;
Yet with your torch you homeward would retire,
And heart'ly wish your bed your fun'ral Pyre.
    With what a fury have I known you feed,
Upon a Contract, and the hopes 't might speed;
Not the fair Bride, impatient of delay,

Doth wish like you the Beauties of that day;
Hotter than all the rosted Cooks you sat
To dresse the fricace of your Alphabet,
Which sometimes would be drawn dough Anagrame,
Sometimes Acrostick parched in the Flame;
Then Posies stew'd with Sippets, motto's by,
Of minced Verse a miserable Pye.
How many knots slip'd ere you twist their name
With th' old device, as both their Heart's the same:
Whilst like to drills the Feast in your false jaw,
You would transmit at leisure to your Maw;
Then after all your fooling, fat, and wine,
Glutton'd at last, return at home to pine.

    Tell me, O Sun, since first your beams did play
To Night, and did awake the sleeping day;
Since first your steeds of Light their race did start,
Did you ere blush as now? Oh thou that art
The common Father to the base Pissmire,
As well as great *Alcides*, did the fire,
From thine owne Altar which the gods adore,
Kindle the Souls of Gnats and Wasps before?

    Who would delight in his chast eyes to see,
Dormise to strike at Lights of Poesie?
Faction and Envy now are downright Rage;
Once a five-knotted whip there was, the Stage:
The Beadle and the Executioner,
To whip small Errors, and the great ones tear.
Now, as er'e *Nimrod* the first King, he writes,
That's strongest, th' ablest deepest bites.
The Muses weeping fly their hill, to see
Their noblest Sons of peace in Mutinie.
Could there nought else this civil war compleat,
But Poets raging with Poetick heat,
Tearing themselves and th' endlesse *wreath*, as though
Immortal they, their wrath should be so too;
And doubly fir'd *Apollo* burns to see
In silent *Helicon* a Naumachie.

Parnassus hears these at his first alarms;
Never till now *Minerva* was in arms.
 O more then Conqu'ror of the *World*, great *Rome*!
Thy *Hero*'s did with gentleness or'e come
Thy Foes themselves, but one another first,
Whilst Envy stript, alone was left, and burst.
The learn'd *Decemviri*, 'tis true did strive,
But to add flames to keep their fame alive;
Whilst the eternal Lawrel hung ith' Air:
Nor of these ten Sons was there found one Heir,
Like to the golden Tripod, it did pass,
From this to this, till 't came to him, whose 't was:
Cæsar to *Gallus* trundled it, and he
To *Maro*: *Maro*, *Naso*, unto thee;
Naso to his *Tibullus* flung the wreath,
He to *Catullus*; thus did each bequeath,
This glorious Circle to another round,
At last the Temples of their God it bound.
 I might believe, at least, that each might have
A quiet fame contented in his Grave,
Envy the living, not the dead, doth bite,
For after death all men receave their right.
If it be Sacriledge for to profane
Their Holy Ashes, what is't then their Flame?
He does that wrong unweeting or in Ire,
As if one should put out the Vestal fire.
 Let Earths four quarters speak, and thou *Sun* bear
Now witnesse for thy Fellow-Traveller,
I was ally'd dear *Uncle* unto thee
In blood, but thou alas not unto me;
Your vertues, pow'rs, and mine differ'd at best,
As they whose Springs you saw, the East and West.
Let me awhile be twisted in thy Shine,
And pay my due devotions at thy Shrine.
 Might learned *Waynman* rise, who went with thee
In thy Heav'ns work beside Divinity,
I should sit still; or mighty *Falkland* stand,

To justifie with breath his pow'rful hand;
The glory that doth circle your pale Urn,
Might hallow'd still and undefiled burn;
But I forbear; Flames that are wildly thrown
At sacred heads, curle back upon their own;
Sleep heav'nly *Sands*, whilst what they do or write,
Is to give God himself and you your right.

    There is not in my mind one sullen Fate
Of old, but is concentred in our state.
Vandall ore-runners, Goths in Literature,
Ploughmen that would *Parnassus* new manure;
Ringers of Verse that All-in All-in chime,
And toll the changes upon every Rhime.
A Mercer now by th' yard does measure ore
An Ode, which was but by the foot before;
Deals you an Ell of Epigram, and swears
It is the strongest and the finest Wears.
No wonder if a Drawer Verses Rack,
If 'tis not his, 't may be the Spir't of Sack;
Whilst the Fair Bar-maid stroaks the Muses teat,
For milk to make the Posset up compleat.

    Arise, thou rev'rend shade, great *Johnson* rise!
Break through thy marble natural disguise;
Behold a mist of Insects, whose meer Breath
Will melt thy hallow'd leaden house of Death.
What was *Crispinus*, that you should defie
The Age for him? He durst not look so high
As your immortal Rod, He still did stand
Honour'd, and held his forehead to thy brand.
These Scorpions with which we have to do,
Are Fiends, not only small but deadly too.
Well mightst thou rive thy Quill up to the Back
And scrue thy Lyre's grave chords, untill they crack.
For though once Hell resented Musick, these
Divels will not, but are in worse disease.
How would thy masc'line Spirit, Father *Ben*,
Sweat to behold basely deposed men,

Justled from the Prerog'tive of their Bed,
Whilst *wives* are per'wig'd with their *husbands head*?
Each snatches the male quill from his faint hand
And must both nobler write and understand,
He to her fury the soft plume doth bow:
O Pen, nere truely justly slit till now!
Now as her self a Poem she doth dresse,
And curls a Line, as she would do a tresse;
Powders a Sonnet as she does her hair,
Then prostitutes them both to publick Aire.
Nor is 't enough that they their faces blind
With a false dye, but they must paint their mind;
In meeter scold, and in scann'd order brawl,
Yet there's one *Sapho* left may save them all.
    But now let me recal my passion,
Oh (from a noble Father, nobler Son!)
You that alone are the *Clarissimi*,
And the whole gen'rous state of *Venice* be,
It shall not be recorded *Sanazar*
Shall boast inthron'd alone this new made star;
You whose correcting Sweetnesse hath forbad
Shame to the good, and glory to the bad,
Whose honour hath ev'n into vertue tam'd,
These Swarms that now so angerly I nam'd.
Forgive what thus distemper'd I indite,
For it is hard a *Satyre* not to write.
Yet as a Virgin that heats all her blood,
At the first motion of bad understood,
Then at meer thought of fair chastity,
Straight cools again the Tempests of her Sea;
    So when to you I my devotions raise,
    All wrath and storms do end in calm and praise.

Notes

p.13. *Lady Anne Lovelace*: née Lady Anne Wentworth, she was the daughter of Thomas Wentworth, 1st earl of Cleveland, and wife of John, 2nd Lord Lovelace of Hurley. Born 1623, she married John in 1638.
Loretto's shrine: a Catholic shrine which is the subject of Marian pilgrimages in Loreto, Italy. The church (the Basilica della Santa Casa) is venerated for enshrining the house in which the Blessed Virgin Mary is popularly believed to have lived. The house is supposed to have been transported to its present location by miraculous intervention, and touched down in Croatia on the way, according to another parallel legend.

15. *Henry Lawes*: (1596–1662) a famous composer of the day, especially renowned for his song settings. His older brother William was also a significant composer. Henry also write the music for Milton's *Comus* and Carew's masque *Coelum Britannicum*.
— *Lucasta*: Lovelace's pet name for the woman he loved, Lucy Sacheverell, whom he called "lux casta" (*Latin*, pure – or chaste – light).

16. *John Laniere*: member of the musical Laniere family, and son of Nicholas Laniere, musician to Queen Elizabeth I in 1581.

17. *Heav'nly Sydney*: refers to Sir Philip Sidney (1554–1586), a major poet of the Elizabethan period who died fighting in the Netherlands, and whose great work, *Arcadia*, was published posthumously by his sister, in 1590.
— *Juno*: queen of the gods; wife of Jupiter.

18. *Amarantha*: a generic "pastoral" name.

20. *Mr Hudson*: identity unclear, but he may be the George Hudson who is recorded as having co-written the music for one of Davenant's plays.

21. *Dr John Wilson*: Wilson (1595–1674) was a renowned lutenist of the day, and a favourite of the King.
— *Flora*: Goddess of flowering plants, and Roman equivalent of the Greek Chloris.
— *Aurora*: goddess of the dawn; *cf* Greek *Eos*.
— *Venus*: Roman goddess of love; Greek Aphrodite.
— *Silenus*: companion to the Greek god Dionysus, who was almost permanently drunk, but was supposed to be able to foretell the future.

22. *Gratiana*: a character in James Shirtley's comedy, *The Wedding* (1629).
— *Atlas*: Greek Titan, who held the sky aloft.

23. *Graces*: three minor goddesses, who symbolised beauty, charm and goodness. Their origins vary according to the tale; in some they are the daughters of Zeus and Hera; in others Zeus and Eurynome, the daughter of Oceanus; or of Helios and Aegle, a daughter of Zeus.
— *Apollo*: one of the most significant gods in the Greco-Roman pantheon, his areas of influence were archery, music and dance, truth and prophecy, healing and diseases, the Sun and light, poetry, and others. The Graces would entertain the gods by dancing to the sound of Apollo's lyre.

24. *Princess Löysa*: Princess Louisa (or Louise) Hollandine of the Palatinate (1622–1709), sixth child and second daughter of Elizabeth Stuart and her husband Frederick V, Elector Palatine and also recently dethroned King of Bohemia. Her brother Rupert was commander of Charles I's armies and was made an Oxford MA at the same time as Lovelace. Louisa was a talented artist, taught by Gerrit van Honthorst, and never married – perhaps because she had little in the way of dowry – and eventually entered a nunnery. Lovelace is likely to have met her at The Hague.
— *Minerva*: Roman goddess of wisdom; equates to Greek Athena.
— *Eccho*: Echo, a nymph "visited" by Zeus, somewhat to the distress of his wife, Hera. For the sin of protecting Zeus from his wife, Echo was cursed so that she could only utter the last words that had been said to her. When she met Narcissus – who famously fell in love with his own reflection – she was unable to express her feelings for him.
— *Syrinx*: a nymph, and follower of Artemis, who was chaste. Pursued by the satyr god, *Pan* – who usually had only one thing on his mind – she went to the river's edge and begged for help from the naiads (river nymphs). She was promptly turned into hollow water reeds, which made a beautiful sound when her frustrated pursuer blew across them. He proceeded to cut the reeds and thus invented the pan-pipes, also known as a *syrinx*.
— *Ariadne*: daughter of the legendary King Minos of Crete; via her mother, Pasiphaë, she was the half-sister of the Minotaur.
— *Anaxarete*: a Greek princess who resisted the advances of the shepherd, *Iphis*, and took her own life.
— *Phoebus*: another of the names of the god, Apollo, god of the Sun, light, oracles, knowledge, healing, diseases, music, poetry, songs, dance, archery, etc, etc.
— *Leucothoë*: there is more than one such in the Greek legends, but this is probably the princess who was a daughter of King Orchamus of Assyria. Sister to Clytia, Leucothoë was loved by Helios, who disguised himself as Leucothoë's mother to gain entrance to her chambers. Clytia, who wanted Helios for herself, told the King the truth, thus betraying her sister's trust. In a temper, Orchamus ordered Leucothoë – who had claimed Helios had forced her to submit to him – buried alive. Helios changed Leucothoë's lifeless body into an incense plant.

— *Daphne*: a dryad (tree-nymph) in Greek mythology. Apollo fell in love with her, being duped into doing so by Cupid's golden arrow after Apollo had insulted him. To add further injury, he shot a leaden arrow at Daphne, so that she could not return Apollo's love. She ran away to the river of which her father Peneus was the god, where Apollo tricked her into disrobing; her father saved her virtue by turning her into a laurel tree. Depending on the version of the myth one prefers, either Daphne gives the love-sick god a laurel wreath, or he takes it in memory of her.
— *bayes*: i.e. laurel leaves, used to crown poets and sportsmen.
— *Adonis*: Greek god of beauty and desire. Aphrodite fell in love with him, protected him and sent him to Persephone to raise as her own. The latter declined to give him back, however, and in the ensuing dispute, Zeus was called upon to adjudicate and ruled that he should spend one third of a year with each goddess, and a final third with whomever he chose. He chose to spend that third with Aphrodite too. He died after being attacked by a wild boar sent by Artemis, who was jealous of his hunting skills; a variant has it that the boar was sent by the god Ares, who was Aphrodite's lover. After his death, Aphrodite mixed nectar into his blood, from which the anemone flower sprang forth.

25 *Princess Katherine*: daughter of King Charles I and Queen Henrietta Maria, she was born and died 29 June 1639. Her name is usually spelled with a C.
— *white Iös*: Io was a priestess of Hera in Argos, after whom Zeus lusted. One version of the myth that her father threw her out of his house, upon the advice of the Oracle, despite her spurning the god's advances. Zeus turns her into a white heifer so as to hide her from his wife; or, Hera transforms her – depending on the version one follows.

26 *cherubin*: cherubim (Hebrew), divine beings, second highest order of angels. Attendants of God, and guardians of the Ark of the Covenant.
— *brother Prince*: Prince Rupert of the Rhine.

27 *seraphins*: seraphim (Hebrew), highest order of angels.

28 *saraband*: a sarabande (Spanish *zarabanda*) is a dance form that may have originated in the Spanish Americas, and is first mentioned in print in 1593. In its early form it was regarded as indecent, but it mutated into a slow courtly dance and, in that form, became popular in France and, later, in England.

32 *Orpheus / Euridice*: in one of the great myths of doomed lovers, Orpheus, son of Apollo and a musician, marries the beautiful Euridice. Hymen, the god of marriage, predicts that the union will not last and indeed, when

fleeing from the advances of a shepherd named Aristæus, Euridice is bitten by a snake and dies. The distraught Orpheus descends into the underworld, and manages to charm Hades, the ruling god there, with his musical skill. Hades permits him to take Euridice back to the world above, on condition that, on the way, he must not look back at his wife. During the journey, he realises that he cannot hear her footsteps and turns around, only to see her there – and of course, he loses her forever. As she was now a spirit, she would have made no sound when walking...
— *Mr Curtes*: obviously a musician, but his identity is unclear.

33 *Charles Cotton*: a poet, for whom Lovelace wrote the nuptial poem, 'The Triumphs of Philamore and Amoret' (see. p.143).
— *Ceres*: Roman goddess of agriculture, grain, and motherly love. Daughter of Saturn, sister of Jupiter, and mother of Proserpine.
— *Bacchus*: Roman god of agriculture, wine and fertility, equivalent to the Greek Dionysus.

34 *Vestall*: i.e. Vestal Virgin — a priestess of the Vesta, Roman goddess of the hearth. They usually came from prominent families, and were sworn to chastity.
— *Ætna*: the volcano, Mount Etna, in Sicily.
— *Hesper*: i.e. Hesperus, the evening star.

35 *John Gamble*: Musician who died in 1687, and published a collection of *Ayres and Dialogues* in 1656, which went into a second edition a year later. He published another volume in 1659. After the Restoration, he joined the royal household and played in the court band.

37 *Ellinda*: identity unclear.
— *Anch'rites*: an anchorite is a religious recluse, or hermit.

39 *Elizabeth Filmer*: daughter of Sir Edward Filmer (d. 1629) and Elizabeth senior (d. 1638). The Filmers were a prominent Kentish family.

45 *Tunbridge / taking the waters*: Tunbridge, Kent, now known as Tunbridge Wells, was a location for medicinal bathing.

47 *Parian*: refers to marble from the Greek island of Paros. *The Parian Marble* (or *Chronicle*) also refers to a Greek chronology, covering the years from 1582–299 BC, inscribed on a stele, which was found on the island of Paros in two parts, and sold in Smyrna in the early 17th century to an agent for Thomas Howard, Earl of Arundel. The inscription on the stele was deciphered by John Selden and published among the *Arundel Marbles, Marmora Arundelliana* (London 1628–29).

48 *Peter Lilly*: Sir Peter Lely, court painter, originally from Soest, in the Netherlands, who came to England with William of Orange. He did well under Charles I but did better still after the Restoration, under Charles II. The finest portraitist in England at the time.
— *picture of His Majesty & Duke of York*: The painting is still extant and is in the collection of the Duke of Northumberland, at Syon House.
— *Hampton-Court*: royal palace on the Thames, south-west of London. The portrait was painted there.

50 *Fletcher reviv'd*: John Fletcher was a Jacobean dramatist who often worked in tandem with Francis Beaumont, and wrote a large number of successful works. The lines here are a commendatory poem printed in the first folio of Beaumont and Fletcher's works in 1647.
— *Ætius*: a Roman general during the late Empire period, and the most successful one of the era, defeating Attila's Huns in 451.
— *Valentinian*: Valentinian I (321–375) was Roman emperor from 364 until his death. He was the last really successful emperor, thanks in part to the services of his great general, Theodosius.
— *Alcides*: another name of Herakles (Roman: Hercules), greatest of the Greek heroes, and a demigod.
— *Bull*: as one of the "labours" that Hercules was forced to undertake, he had to capture the Cretan bull, father of the Minotaur.

51 *Minerva*: see note to page 23 above.
— *Venus*: see note to page 20 above.
— *Cupid*: Eros in his Greek guise, he was the god of desire and erotic love. Also known as *Amor* (Latin for "love").
— *Diana*: Roman goddess of hunting (Greek: Artemis).

52 *Hermes*: Greek messenger god (Roman: Mercury).
— *Lady A L*: Anne, Lady Lovelace.

55 *The Scholars*: comedy written by Lovelace. It was performed at Salisbury Court, previously known as the Whitefriars playhouse – the latter closed in 1621.

56 *Proteus*: prophetic sea-god, and "old man of the sea", according to Homer. He was able to change shape to avoid capture. This versatility gives rise to our modern adjective, "protean".

57 *Clitophon, Lucippe*: star-crossed lovers in an ancient Greek romance, dating to the 2nd century AD.
— *Sydney's Arcady*: the *Arcadia* of Sir Philip Sidney, published in 1590.

58 *Pamela*: the heroine of the *Arcadia*.
— *Cariclea*: character in another Greek Romance, the *Aethiopica*, or *Theagenes and Chariclea*, written by Heliodorus. It was first translated into English in 1569 by Thomas Underdown, who used the 1551 Latin translation of Stanisław Warszewicki to create his *Aethiopian Historie*.
— *Astrea*: virgin Greek goddess of justice, innocence, purity and precision. According to Ovid, Astræa abandoned the earth during the Iron Age. Fleeing from the new wickedness of humanity, she ascended to heaven to become the constellation Virgo. Lovelace is probably referring however to the French Romance, *L'Astrée*, published in four parts between 1610 and 1618.
— *Hellens*: i.e. Hellenes, Greeks.

59 *My… valiant Freind*: a commendatory poem that preceded *Pallas Armata: The Gentlemans Armorie*, a sword-fighting manual, published in 1639.
— *Amyntor, Chloris, Arigo, Gratiana*: the 1971 Oxford Authors edition of Lovelace's poems offers an interpretation of these names as being pseudonyms for Endymion Porter (Amyntor), his wife Olivia (Chloris), and two of his children (Arigo and Gratiana).

60 *Titian, Raphael, Georgone*: Italian masters whose paintings all figured in the Royal collection; Porter frequently acquired paintings for Charles I, and may have owned some himself, as he was a patron of Van Dyck and Rubens. The name of the last of the three painters is correctly spelled Giorgione.

63 *Semele*: in a Greek myth dating back to Mycenean times, Semele was the youngest daughter of Cadmus and Harmonia, and was the mother of Dionysus by Zeus in one of the Dionysian origin myths. The reference here is to the story that when Zeus appeared to Semele and told her who he was, she refused to believe him and demanded some proof. She was consumed in the fires caused by his lightning bolts, even though he had tried to reduce their power.
— *Purple-roabe*: signifies royalty, or imperial power.

64 *booreinn*: literally, a female boor, perhaps a peasant.

66 *To Althea*: the most famous of Lovelace's poems, apparently written while he was imprisoned in the Gatehouse in 1642.
— *Dr John Wilson*: English composer and lutenist. Active at the Caroline court, and again later in the Restoration court.

67 *coran*: Koran or Al'Quran.
— *elles of beere*: an ell was a measurement, amounting to 45 inches. This phrase thus suggests a "yard of ale".

— *flutes of Canary*: tall slim glasses of sparkling wine.
— *pasties-Mary*: marrow.

68 *Hans… Kelder*: from the Dutch phrase *Hans-en-kelder*, commonly translated into English as "Jack-in-the-cellar".
— *Amadis*: Amadis de Gaula, hero of Montalvo's late-15th-century or early 16th-century Spanish romance, published in an English translation by Anthony Munday in 1590. There were also a number of French translations that Lovelace might have seen.
— *Sir Guy*: Guy, Earl of Warwick, hero of an English Romance, dating back to the 13th century. A manuscript version in English survives from the early 14th century. Lovelace is likely to have known one of the more recent iterations of the story, by John Lane (1617) or Samuel Rowlands (1607), Sir Guy is mentioned in passing in Shakespeare's *Henry VIII* (Porter's Man: "I am not Samson, nor Sir Guy, nor Colbrand, To mow 'em down before me.").
— *Topaz*: Sir Topaz, another hero of Romance.
— *Generall Goring*: Lord Goring (1608–1657) was the eldest son of the 1st Earl of Norwich, and had a reputation as a dissolute. While he seemed to have some ability as a soldier, his forces were soundly defeated in the West of England by Fairfax's parliamentary forces, and he left the country, eventually taking up a military position in the Spanish army. He died in Madrid in 1657, a Catholic convert.
— *pacification at Berwicke*: the Treaty of Berwick (1639), was a truce – temporary, as it turned out – between England and Scotland, after some hostilities between them.

69 *A la Chabot*: *La chabot* was a French dance tune named after the Admiral. *The Tragedy of Chabot, Admiral of France*, a play by George Chapman, was published in 1639, and first performed at some point between 1635 and 1638 at London's Cockpit Theatre.
— *Lettice*: Lettice Boyle, wife of Lord Goring.
— *Sir Thomas Wortley*: younger brother of the better-known Sir Francis, another Cavalier poet.

73 *Brother Colonel F.L.*: the author's brother, Francis.
— *Brothers untimely death at Carmarthen*. The incident occurred in 1644. The brother is William, who must have been fighting under his elder brother's command.

74 *Mrs Cassandra Cotton*: the author's aunt, and sister to Charles Cotton.
— *Mr C Cotton*: Charles Cotton.

76 *Epode*: probably refers to Horace's use of the form (written in couplets), rather than the Greek original, which was the third section of an ode.

77 *Bilingsgate*: Billingsgate, a gate and landing place for goods on the Thames.

78 *Dido*: Queen of Carthage in Virgil's *Aeneid*, and the lover of the hero, Aeneas. She committed suicide after Aeneas abandoned her.
— *Phaeton*: Apollo's carriage.
— *axel-tree*: axle; the bar onto which two opposete wheels of a cart or carriage are fastened.
— *Ulisses*: = Odysseus, King of Ithaca, and hero of the *Odyssey*.
— *Saint Syren*: siren.
— *Philomel*: daughter of Pandion, King of Athens. She was turned into a swallow and her sister Procne into a nightingale when they were being pursued by the evil Tereus, who had married Procne and raped Philomel.

82 brave Tamyris: Tomyris, 6th century BC queen of the Massagetae, a Scythian tribe. She led her armies in battle and defeated the Persian Emperor, Cyrus, killing him, according to Herodotus.

83 *A la Bourbon done moy plus de pitié ou plus de cruaulté, car sans ci le ne puis pas vivre, ne morir* (French): To the Bourbon Rose, give me more pity, or else more cruelty, for without this I can neither live, nor die. (The rose was probably named in honour of the ruling house of France.)

88 Cousin A.L.: Anne Lovelace.

89 *Cimmerian*: a nomadic people from the Pontic steppe region, whose name gave rise to the area we call Crimea today.

92 *Heliotropian*: Heliotrope was the name for the sunflower, or indeed, any flower that turns and follows the sun.

94 *Io and Europa's bull*: see note to p. 25 above.

98 *Paphos*: coastal city on Cyprus.
— *Queene of Love*: Venus.

100 *Hydraphil*: lover of the hydra (a many-headed beast) – this may be a coded reference to the Puritan "enemy".
— *Philanact*: likewise may be a coded reference to "cavaliers".

103 *'N'entendez vous pas ce language'* (French): 'Do you not understand this language?'
— *Echo*: see note to p.23 above.

110 *Galliard*: a popular dance form.
— *Saraband*: another dance. See note to p. 28 above.

111 *Zephyr*: from the Greek meaning the west wind. Later in the 17th century it came to mean "a gentle breeze".

112 *Inde*: India.

113 *Cato*: an orator and politician (95–46 BC) in ancient Rome, who was a constant enemy of Julius Caesar,a nd opponent of the first Triumvirate (Caesar, Pompey & Crassus). In the end he committed suicide rather than live under Caesar's rule.
— *Margaret Pie*: i.e. magpie.
— *Sir John Daw*: i.e. jackdaw

114 *Euclid*: Greek mathematician, and creator of the discipline of Geometry.
Phoebus: Apollo

115 *Scythians*: a nomadic people of the Pontic steppe region; their language was related to old Persian. The term tends to be used as a catch-all for nomadic warrior tribes. Lovelace would have known of them from Herodotus.

116 *Centaur*: mythical Greek being, half man and half horse.
— *Syren*: siren — beautiful women who would call to passing sailors, tempting them to join them; best known for their appearance in the *Odyssey*, where they tempted Odysseus. Hence, "siren-call" or "siren-song".
— *Hermaphrodite*: character in Ovid's *Metamorphoses*.
— *Trevere*: this may be the town of Vere on the island of Walcheren, near Flushing (Vlissingen).
— *Huyck*: huke, a kind of woman's gown.

117 *Courante*: a dance.
— *Saraband*: see note to p. 28 above
— *Vestal*: see note to p. 34 above
— *Canary*: see note to page 68 above.
— *Rhenish*: white wine from the Rhine region in Germany.
— *posset*: a dessert made of lemon, cream, sugar and egg.

119 *penons*: i.e. pennants: banners with a triangular end.
— *Cousin-german*: = cousin. The word cousin was often used for looser relationships; in this case a blood relative is meant, in the modern sense of "cousin".

120 *Spannels*: spaniels, dogs.
— *Epicedium*: a funeral ode.

122 *Hobby*: a kind of hawk.
— *Lanner, Lanneret, Goshawk, Tercel*: hawks; the first three are different types of hawk, while the last-named means the male of any of them.
— *Pye*: magpie.

126 *Cassiopea*: a constellation; before her ascent into the heavens she was the Queen of Ethiopia and mother of Andromeda.

127 *Castara*: a book published anonymously in 1634. The name seems to refer to Lucy Herbert, younger daughter of William Herbert, 1st Lord Powys, who married William Habington, a poet, in 1630.
— *Aurum Fulminans*: fulminate of gold, an explosive compound made by adding ammonia to a solution of auric chloride.
— *Paulina*: famously extravagant wife of Gaius. Her story is related by Pliny.

128 *Don-Quichoterie*: quixotry. *Don Quixote* was published in English translation in 1612 (Book 1) and 1620 (Book 2). As the French transcription *Don Quichotte* suggests, in 17th century Spanish the 'x' in Quixote was soft, like English 'sh' in "wash".

129 *Cybele*: a Greek goddess with Anatolian origins. She was adopted by the Romans as a mother goddess (*Magna Mater*).
— *Jove*: also Jupiter, (Greek: Zeus), King of the gods.
— *Psyche*: princess of great beauty who aroused the jealousy of Venus and the love of Cupid. Apuleius recounts the story in *The Golden Ass*.
— *Mercurie*: Mercury, the messenger god.
— *Juno*: queen of the Gods, wife of Jupiter.

130 *Cerberus*: Cerberus, the three-headed dog that guarded the entry to Hades. *Whitehall*: the Palace of Whitehall was the King's main residence. The banqueting hall is the only part that survives today, after the great fire of the late 17th century.
— *Charon*: the ferryman who rowed dead souls across the river Styx on their way to Hades.
— *Tarquin*: the name of the last three Kings of ancient Rome, the last of whom died in 496 BC. Charles II was often referred to by this name.
— *Oliver-Brutus*: Cromwell.
— *spent-gorge*: possibly means that throats have been emptied after being cut;

131 *Hony Soit*: the beginning of the famous motto of the Order of the Garter,

Honi soit qui mal y pense (Old French, meaning, more or less: "shame be upon him that evil thinks").

133 *Acheron*: the River of Woe in Greek mythology, and one of the five rivers of the Underworld. In Homer, it is a river of Hades, and in Virgil's work, it i33s the source from which the Styx arises.
— *Hymen*: god of marriage.
— *Flambeau*: a burning torch.
— *Vestal*: see note to p. 34 above
— *Limbecks*: old form of *alembics*. An early chemical vessel used to purify substances through distillation.

134 Curtius: probably the 1st-century Roman historian, Quintus Curtius Rufus, author of the *Histories of Alexander the Great*.
— *Auricular*: related to hearing.

136 *Elizian*: Elysian; i.e. related to Heaven.

137 *Rhadamant*: Rhadamanthus or Rhadamanthys was a King of Crete. Along with his brother, Minos, he became one of the three judges of the dead in the Underworld.
— *Arachne*: was a weaver who was so skilful that she dared to challenge Athena, goddess of war and handicraft. Athena wove a tapestry that showed the gods in all their majesty, while Arachne's effort showed their amorous adventures. Enraged her rival's work (either because it was irreverent, or because it was too good), Athena ripped it up, and Arachne hanged herself out of despair. But Athena then loosened the rope, which turned into a cobweb; Arachne was turned into a spider, hence the name *Arachnid*. Ovid's *Metamorphoses* is the main source.

138 *Naumachie*: naumachia, naval battle.
3— *charact*: carrack, an armed merchant vessel of an original Italian design, but updated by the Portuguese. The design was familiar to the English through Hakluyt's detailed description.

139 *Stygian*: i.e. of the Styx; dark.
— *Sphynx*: sphinx; a mythical creature with the head of a human and the body of a lion.

141 *Hellebore*: flowering plant, also known as Lenten-rose or Christmas-rose.
— *Pallas*: the goddess Athena (see also *Arachne*, note to p. 138 above).

143 *Charles Cotton*: (1630–1687), minor poet, translator of Montaigne's *Essays*, friend of Izaak Walton, and contributor to the latter's *The Compleat Angler*.

— *Mæcha*: Mecca, the Muslim holy city and goal of pilgrimage.
— *Regulus*: probably Marcus Aquilius Regulus, a 1st-century Roman senator, and notorious informer, who was active during the reigns of Emperors Nero and Domitian. Pliny, Tacitus and Martial all wrote about him.

143 *Philamore*: the implies that he loves love – a conflation of Greek *philo* and Latin *amor*.
— *Amoret*: the name implies love, as in Old French *amorette*. The poem was written as a wedding gift, an epithalamium, for Lovelace's friend, Charles Cotton.

144 *Ducaleon*: There is more than one such person in the myths, but this is likely to be the Deucalion from the Greek myth of the Flood, whose ark comes to rest on the slopes of Mt. Parnassus. The story is related in Ovid's *Metamorphoses*.
— *a la Mode*: *à la mode* (French): fashionable.
— *Ariadne*: was a Cretan princess in Greek mythology. Associated with mazes and labyrinths because of her part in the story of Theseus and the Minotaur.
— *piacle*: sacrificial offering.

145 *Boötes*: star constellation, known to the ancients, and described by Ptolemy.
— *Neptune*: god of the sea.
— *Thetis*: sea-goddess and leader of the sea-nymphs, the Nereids. Mother of Achilles.

147 *Francis Lovelace*: the poet's younger brother (1621–1675), later the second governor of colonial New York. During his tenure, he purchased Staten Island from the native Americans, and ran a tavern, The King's House, in lower Manhattan. The foundations can be seen today on Pearl Street.

148 *Dione*: Diana, the huntress-goddess.
— *Galileo*: Galileo Galilei (1564–1642), famous astronomer and physicist, who caused himself grief by pointing out that the world was round and also that it revolved around the sun, both of which were contrary to official teachings. The Inquisition was unimpressed by this and he was forced to abjure his findings, and spent his last years under house arrest.
— *Ixion*: King of the Lapiths, a Thessalian tribe, and one of the sons of Ares.

149 *Aeolus*: in the *Odyssey* and the *Aeneid*, the Keeper of the Winds.
— *sleeping Nine*: the Muses.

150 *Thomas Stanley*: poet and translator (1625–1678). A distant relative of Lovelace.

151 *Io* and *Ox*: see note to p. 25 above.
— *Paris' Judgement*: in Greek mythology, Paris of Troy had to judge which of three goddesses, Hera, Athena, and Aphrodite, was the most beautiful. Paris could not make a decision, but when they removed their clothes in a final attempt to convince him, things changed. Each of the three also tried to bribe young Paris, and the winning bribe – or combination of bribe and beauty – was that of Aphrodite, who promised to secure for him the most beautiful woman in the world. This was Helen, Queen of Sparta, whose elopement with Paris was the cause of the Trojan War in the *Iliad*. The judgement was a popular theme with painters, who thus had an excuse to paint three naked women.
— *R. Caesar*: Robert Caesar was the son of Sir Julius Caesar [sic], Master of the Rolls, and later Chancellor of the Exchequer under James I. The unusual name comes from Sir Julius' father, an Italian doctor, and graduate of the University of Padua by name of Cesare Adelmare. (Sir Julius was also known as Adelmare.) Robert was married to Lovelace's sister Johanna.

152 *Peter Lilly*: see note to p. 48 above.

154 *Titiam*: Titian (1490–1576), Venetian painter.
— *Charls*; the King.
— *Holbeen*: Hans Holbein, German painter, and court painter to Henry VIII.
— *Henry*: King Henry VIII.
— *Vasari*: Italian artist of the 16th century and author of the *Lives of the Artists*.
— *Vermander*: Carl Vermander (or Ver Mander), an early Dutch commentator on art.

155 *Picts*: Lovelace seems to mean "painters" with this, from the Latin for "painted", *picti* in the plural.
— *Eldred Revett*: early 17th-century poet. His *Poems* were published in 1657. he wrote an elegy on Lovelace after the latter's death.

156 *Aeson*: King of Iolcus in Thessaly; father to Jason (of the Argonauts).
— *Rod of Aaron*: refers to the Biblical miracle story of the flowering rod. (*Numbers* 17; *Hebrews* 9:4).
— *Nestor*: King of Pylos, mentioned in the *Odyssey*.

157 *John Gamble*: Composer active at the English court. Died 1687.

158 *Urania*: one of the Muses, her province was astronomy.
— *Amphion*: there are several people with this name in mythology, but this one might be the one from the Argonauts story.
— *Ut re mi*: in the solfège (or sol-fa) system, the first three notes. The names

of the notes were derived by Guido d'Arezzo from the initial letters of each strophe of the Latin hymn, 'Ut queant laxis'.
— *Fletcher*: John Fletcher (1579–1625), English playwright.
— *Wild Goose Chase*: play by Fletcher (1621)

158 *Three Kingdomes*: refers to the split of the Roman empire into three, under the triumvirs Octavian (later Augustus), Mark Antony and Marcus Lepidus.
— *Antony*: Mark Antony, triumvir, and lover of Cleopatra.

160 *Aspatia*: a character in *The Maid's Tragedy*, a play by Beaumont and Fletcher (1619).
— *Dr F Beale*: Francis Beale (dates uncertain), author of the *Royall Game of Chesse Play* (1656).
— *John Hall*: (1627–1656), poet and pamphleteer.
— *Hierocles*: 5th century writer whose only extant work is a commentary on the *Golden Verses* of Pythagoras. Halls' version was published posthumously in 1657.
— *Castriot*: George Castriot, King Skanderbeg of Albania.
— *Swisse*: = Swiss, as in the Swiss guards of the Vatican.

161 *praetextat*: juvenile, or junior.
— *Ferula*: (Latin) rod, Imperial sceptre.
— *Cam*: the river in Cambridge, thus alluding to Hall's student days.
— *Tully*: i.e. Marcus Tullius Cicero, the Roman orator.

162 *Clarissimi*: the "famous men"; this was an epithet borne by all Roman senators.
— *hexastick*: hexastich, a poem, or stanza, of six lines.
— *Lepanto*: the Battle of Lepanto (1571) was where the western powers defeated the Ottoman forces.
— *Turbants*: turbans, head-dress, worn by Turkish men.
— *Candie*: The Kingdom of Candia, the Italian name for Crete when it was a Venetian colony. Ottoman forces took most of the island during the Cretan War (1645–1669), but the eponymous city of Candia (modern Heraklion) held out, along with two other fortresses. These were eventually to fall to the Ottomans in 1715.

163 *Lucan*: 1st-century Roman poet, Marcus Annaeus Lucanus.

164 *Diogenes*: 4th-century BC Greek philosopher and Cynic.
— *Aretine*: Pietro Aretino (1492–1556), Italian poet and author.

165 *Thebes*: ancient Greek city in Boeotia, and leader of the Boeotian confederacy, whose origins stretch back to Mycenaean times. A major rival of

Athens, and victor over Sparta in 371 BC, the city was destroyed by Alexander the Great. Site of the stories of Cadmus, Oedipus, Dionysus, Herakles and others.
— *Troy*: the opponent of the Greeks in the Trojan Wars related in the *Iliad*.
— *Maccaroon*: a buffoon, or a fop.

166 *Alcides*: also known as Herakles, or Hercules, the demigod famed for his strength.
— *Nimrod*: Biblical figure said to be King of Shinar in Mesopotamia; builder of the Tower of Babel, according to other traditions.
— *Helicon*: mountain in Greece, and location of two springs sacred to the Muses. Serves as an emblem of poetic inspiration.

167 *Minerva*: Roman goddess of wisdom.
— *Decemviri*: a special commission of ten men in ancient Rome; invariably refers to the commission that drew up Rome's first code of law.
— *Maro*: surname of Ovid.
— *Naso*: surname of Virgil.
— *Tibullus*: 1st-century BC Latin writer of elegies.
— *Catullues*: i.e. Catullus, Roman poet.
— *Sandys*: the author's great-uncle, George Sandys (1578–1644).
— *Waynman*: Sir Francis Wenman, husband to Sandys' niece; or, possibly Thomas Wenman (1596–1665), 2nd Viscount Wenman and a minor poet.
— *Falkland*: Lucius Cary, 2nd Viscount Falkland (1610–1643), poet.

168 *Sands*: see *Sandys* above.
— *Parnassus*: mountain in Greece, home of the Muses.
— *Johnson*: Ben Jonson.
— *Crispinus*: a character from Jonson's *Poetaster*. The name alludes to St. Crispin, who was somewhat light-fingered.
— *father Ben*: Ben Jonson.

169 *Sapho*: = Sappho, Greek woman lyric poet from Lesbos, accounted one of the greatest of all Greek poets during the early era. The author may be referring obliquely to the admired woman poet, Katherine Phillips, whose work was only to be published in the 1660s, although manuscripts had long been in circulation, and would have been seen by Lovelace and those in his circle.
— *Clarissimi*: see note to p. 162 above.
— *Sanazar*: Jacopo Sannazaro (1458–1530), Italian writer, most famous for his *Arcadia*.

www.ingramcontent.com/pod-product-compliance
Lightning Source LLC
Chambersburg PA
CBHW022010160426
43197CB00007B/369